Buddhism in China

Ling Haicheng

CHINA INTERCONTINENTAL PRESS

TABLE OF CONTENTS

Chapter Three   Tibetan Buddhism in China

Chapter Four   Pali Language Buddhism of China

Chapter V Buddhism in Contemporary China

INTRODUCTION

Buddhism is a worldwide region. It was originated in India and has developed in China. Of the three major schools of Buddhism, namely, Pali Buddhism, Han Buddhism and Tibetan Buddhism, the latter two were originated in China. China is the only country in the world where the three major schools of Buddhism co-exit, hence the name as the second home to Buddhism. Now the three major schools of Buddhism are found in many parts of the world. Buddhism believers of different skin colors, different nationalities, different ethnicities and different languages all regard China as the ancestral hall of Buddhism. Many of them travel a long way to China to pay homage to the ancestral hall of the Chan sect of Buddhism, the ancestral hall of the pure land sect of Buddhism, the ancestral hall of the Saskapa and the ancestral hall of the Bkabrgyudpa sect ......

Some of the pictures in the book show the magnificent scenes of grand services with an attendance of several thousand and even hundreds of thousands of Buddhists. This is but a mini epitome of the real religious life in China.

It is already 2,000 years since Buddhism spread into China. Chinese Buddhists have contributed greatly to enriching Buddhism. They have not only translated a large amount of Sanskrit scriptures and compiled the great "Tripitaka" but also created such cultural treasures as caves, sculptures, temples and monasteries and other Buddhist arts. Although Chinese Buddhism has experienced a number of disasters and even calamities, it is still living on.

The past decade has witnessed a rapid development of Buddhism. This book gives a brief introduction to the history of Buddhism and more to the current status of this religion in China. It covers both ancient legacies and innovations in the present-day.

Chapter One
Origin and Spread of Chinese Buddhism

1. Origin of Chinese Buddhism

Legend has it that Emperor Ming of the Eastern Han Dynasty (AD 64) had a dream one day of a flying golden deity with a light ring over the bald head. The second day, he summoned his officials and asked them who that giant was. An official named Fu Yi, who was known to be a person who knew all strange things, told the emperor that there was a person known as Buddha in the west, who was very tall, had golden skin and a light ring over his bald head. Emperor Ming felt that he should not take it lightly and dispatched emissaries headed by Cai Yin to the western area to seek dharma or the law. What the omnipotent

◎ Standing Buddha [as Siddhartha], Kushan period, 2nd-3rd century A.D., Gandhara style, schist, measuring 114 x 39 x 18 (cm), now in the New Delhi Museum of India.

Buddha mentioned by Fu Yi was in fact Sakyamuni, the founder of Buddhism.

Sakyamuni was born the son of Suddhodana, of the ksatriya caste, ruler of Kapilavastu, and Maya his wife in the 5th century BC; his personal name was Siddhartha, or Sarvarthasiddha. Later, he became the founder of Buddhism. As the sage and the enlightened one of the Sakya clan, he began his activities to spread Buddhism at the age of 45 until his death at the age of 80.

Buddhism in the Sakyamuni time was primitive, preaching Four Noble Truths (namely, the suffering of life, the origin of the suffering, the cessation of the suffering and the way that leads to this cessation), Noble Eightfold Path (namely, the right view, the right thought, the right speech, the right action, the right living, the right effort, the right mindfulness, and the right concentration), and the twelve nidanas, twelve links in the chain of existence: (1) Ignorance or unenlightenment; (2) action; (3) consciousness; (4) name and form; (5) the six sense organs; (6)contact, touch; (7) sensation, feeling; (8) thirst, desire, craving; (9) laying hold of, grasping; (10) being, existing; (11) birth; (12) old age, death.). While preaching the law, the Buddha established the ranks of monks and places of enlightenment. What the scriptures often mention such as Jetavana vihara, venuvana vihara or 'bamboo-

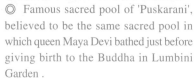

◎ Famous sacred pool of 'Puskarani', believed to be the same sacred pool in which queen Maya Devi bathed just before giving birth to the Buddha in Lumbini Garden .

◎ Bodhgaya Pagoda.

grove vihara were all the most famous places of enlightenment. When Sakyamuni was alive, he taught many doctrines and the rules. But there were no written records. After the death of the Buddha, his disciples carried out the collection and fixing of the Buddhist canon on four occasions, which were called assemblies. The first assembly which gathered to recite the scriptures took place at the Pippala cave at Rajagrha under Ajatasatru, with notable three disciples of Kasyapa, Ananda and Upali attending together with 500 other disciples. The procedure was that some disciples recited the doctrines and rules and after that the attendants would confirm them and then those that reached consensus were written down to become Buddhist scriptures. Such activity to collect and fix Buddhist canon was of major importance in passing on the Buddhist doctrines and rules. There were another two or three similar assemblies in the ensuing 100-200 years. Although the assemblies led to the split into sects, they contributed to the development of Buddhism.

In 271 B.C., the third generation King of MAURYA of ancient India, King Asoka, came to power and encouraged the spread of Buddhism. He did not only order the setup of a special organization charged with the task of spreading Buddhism but also built Buddhist temples and pagodas and sent many senior monks far and wide to disseminate Buddhism. Buddhism was spread at the time mainly along three lines: Sri Lanka to the south, Myanmar to the east and Kashmir and northern Pakistan and the southeastern part of Afghanistan to the north. On the northern line, there was the Kusana Dynasty (50-300) whose ruling line descended from the Yue Zhi, a people, as nomads living in the western part of Gansu Province, Northwest China, at the beginning of the 2nd century BC and later ruled over most of the northern Indian subcontinent, Afghanistan, and parts of Central Asia. The support given by the Indo-Scythian King Kaniska III of the Kushan (Kusana) dynasty (78-120 C.E.), a Buddhist convert, supported Buddhist expansion within a vast region that extended far into the Central Asian heartland and into Xinjiang of China.

Sakyamuni's experience is marked by four major stages. One is birth. After '500 or 550' previous incarnations, Sakyamuni finally attained to the state of Bodhisattva, was born in the Tusita heaven, and descended as a white elephant, through her right side, into the womb of the immaculate Maya, the purest woman on earth; this was on the 8th day of the 4th month; next year on the 8th day of the 2nd month he was born from her right side painlessly as she stood under a tree in the Lumbini garden. Lumbini has thus become the No. 1 sacred place of Buddhism. The second stage of his life is enlightenment. Although born a prince, he was filled with sympathy from childhood. Seven days after he was born, his mother Maya died, leaving him to be brought up by her sister Prajapati; During a ride he first became aware of human suffering in shape of a sick person, an old man and a funeral. Very upset by these visions of true life, Siddharta left his family and for seven years lived as an ascetic, only to find out that the extreme ascetic life was not able to solve the problem of human suffering. Although in due course he was married to Yasodhara who bore him a son, he left home in search of truth, became an ascetic, severely disciplined himself, and finally at the age of 35, under a fig tree ("Bodhi tree), realized

that the way of release from the chain of rebirth and death lay not in asceticism but in moral purity. His third stage is the first discourse, turning of the dharmacakra, the Wheel of the Law. After he became a Buddha, he told his five disciples the truth that dawned on him at a deer park. The deer park has thus become the third sacred place of Buddhism. The last stage is to enter the nirvana, which is regarded as the supreme realm of the

◎ Nativity scene. It is believed that it depicts Maya Devi with her right hand holding on to a sal tree with a newborn child standing upright on a lotus petal, shedding an oval halo, around his head while two celestial figures pour water and lotuses from vessels of heaven as indicated by the delineation of clouds. This nativity scene sculpture is believed to be a work of the 2nd century.

◎ Wheel of the Law Pagoda at Mrgadava, a deer park.

◎ Kusinara - a place where the Buddha, Sakyamuni, died.

world. The Buddha died under a dual Sala-tree in Kusinara, which has become the last sacred place of Buddhism.

Lumbini has been established by Buddhist circles of all countries as the No. 1 sacred place of Buddhism. With the support of UNESCO, Lumbini has set up a development committee. Now, China, Nepal, India, Sri Lanka, Myanmar, Thailand, France, Germany, Vietnam, the Republic of Korea and Japan have built their respective Buddhist temples in Lumbini. The magnificent temple built by China is called Zhong Hua Temple (All-China Temple) with money earmarked by the Chinese government. A ceremony of opening the eyes of the Buddha image was held after its completion on May 27, 2000. The Chinese Buddhist Association sent eight monks and one management person to the temple. This is the first Buddhist temple built by China outside its territory, thus becoming a window to Chinese Buddhism.

2. Introduction of Buddhism into China

There is a very popular Chinese story about monk Tang San Zhang to India to fetch the Buddhist scriptures (628 AD). It is indeed true that Monk Xuan Zhuang went to the western area to fetch Buddhist scriptures and he was the man who brought home the largest amount of scriptures. But he was not the first who did so. The earliest expedition in quest of texts of Buddhist scriptures took place at least seven centuries earlier.

In the last section, we mentioned the dream of Emperor Ming of the Han dynasty and the man, Cai Yin, sent by the emperor to seek the Buddha. It was said that Cai met Kasyapa-Matanga and his companion Gobharana in the western area of China and invited them to Luoyang in the present-day Henan Province. Matanga was said to know all about Buddhist classics and often went to states in the western area to disseminate Buddhism. Story has it that he used the canon of Buddhism to persuade two warring factions into peace. After Matanga arrived in Luoyang, Emperor Ming treated him with great ceremony and invited him to translate Buddhist scriptures at the White-Horse Temple outside the western gate of Luoyang City. He and his companion Gobharana translated a lot of Buddhist scriptures. The first works completed was what is known as the Sutra of the Forty-two Sections. The works passed on till today and occupies an important position in the history of Chinese Buddhism. The Sutra is compiled with some extracts from various Sutras. It consists of basic Buddhist teachings, particularly the moral ones, in order to be assimilated more easily in China. When Cai Yin met the two Indian monks, he also found a painted image of

◎ White-Horse Temple in Luoyang, Henan Province, the earliest Buddhist temple in China.

Sakyamuni and he took it back to Luoyang. Emperor Ming recognized that that was the very golden flying deity with a light ring over the bald head that appeared in his dream and he ordered a painter to paint another copy for worshiping. This is believed to be the first Buddhist image in China.

But the first Chinese monk who went to the western areas to seek the Buddhist teachings was said to be Zhu Shixing of the Three Kingdoms period. Zhu was a native of Yuxian County, Henan Province. He became a monk when very young. He is believed to be the first to take vows to undertake the commandments and officially became a Bhiksu or a monk. So Zhu Shixing is regarded as the first Chinese monk in the history of Chinese Buddhism. In the course of studying Buddhist classics, he felt that the translations of some Buddhist scriptures were not accurate enough and decided to go to the western areas in quest of the originals. In 260, he took the trouble of arduous journey to Yudian (the present-day Hotan in Xinjiang). There he found the long-desired prajnaparamita sutra in the Sanskrit original. It has 90 chapters, running up to more than 600,000 words. But Zhu did not go any further west; neither did he return home. Instead, he asked others to take the Buddhist scriptures home before he died in Yudian.

But the first Chinese who really went the hometown of Sakyamuni in quest of Buddhist teachings is Mong Fa Xian (Fa Hsien) which means "illustrious master of the law, of the Eastern Jin Dynasty, as the history of Buddhism recognizes. With a secular name of Gong, Fa Xian was a native of Wuyang of Pingyang Prefecture (the present-day Qiuxian County, Xiangyang Prefecture of Shanxi Province). He had three elder brothers who all died young. Fearing that he would, too, die in infancy, his father followed the local traditional practice of sending the three-year-old Fa Xian to a temple to undertake the ten commandments of sramanera; but he was too young to be left in the temple alone and had to be brought home. A few years later, Fa Xian caught a serious ill, almost at the verge of dying. He was then sent back to the temple. In the third day after he returned to the temple, he was magically recovered. From then on, he refused to leave the temple. His mother had to buy a small house near the temple in order to take care of him. After he became a monk, he immersed himself in the reading of Buddhist scriptures. Gradually, he found that the translations were incomplete and was determined to learn about Buddhist traditions in India and to discover authentic Buddhist writings. In 399, together with his fellow monks Hui Jing, Dao Zheng, Hui Ying and Hui Sui, he set off on his journey to India. They traveled through the vast shifting sand and lifeless desert. Despite his age and illness, he persisted in the harsh natural conditions. He was grieved over the death of his fellow monk Hui Ying, who died of a disease and Hui Jing who died of cold on the way. Only he and Dao Zheng, whom he met on the way, continued the westward journey. They at last arrived at the northern border of India. It was 402. They visited as many Buddhist sacred shrines as they could, especially those associated with the presence of the Buddha. Fa Xian studied hard Sanscrit, copied canonic teachings and painted Buddha images. He arrived at Celon (Sri Lanka) in 409. It took him 15 years to complete the journey of more than 30 countries. He recovered a large quantity of Buddhist writings and returned to China in 412 and then devoted the rest of his life to translating them. He is regarded as one of the greatest monks in the history of Chinese Buddhism. Fa Xian also wrote a book, which was later translated as A Record of the Buddhistic Kingdoms. The book has received a high appraisal from historians, geographers, archaeologists and Buddhists in the world.

Another great monk who made great contributions to the introduction of Buddhism into China was monk Xuan Zhuang of the Tang Dynasty.

Chapter Two
Han-Language Buddhism in China

Han-language Buddhism refers to the Buddha's religion spreading in areas inhabited by the Han nationality in the first century as the Buddhist teachings were translated from Sanskrit into the Han language and mingled with the Han culture. Up to the Southern and Northern dynasties, outstanding monks and Buddhist scholars made substantial progress in the translation of Buddhist teachings. They translated almost all the works of different sects of Indian Buddhism. But different interpretations of the teachings led to different schools of Buddhism, which was called "Shi" or "Jia" during the Southern and Northern dynasties.

Buddhism was in for its golden age in the Sui and Tang dynasties, when different schools of thought were quite active and getting mature. Many temples were built and famous monks at home and abroad were invited to translate sutras. The

15

outstanding Tang monks made unprecedented achievements in Buddhism study and research. Then Buddhism began to split into different sects, which, in the course of development, evolved into eight major schools: Tiantai, Sanlun, Ci'en, Lu, Huayan, Mi, Jingtu and Chan. These major sects or schools of Buddhism exerted great influence in the 1000-year history of Han language Buddhism. All the important Buddhist teachings were contained in the major schools. The Jingtu Sect or pureland sect and Chan Sect (dhyana in Sanskrit) have remained the mainstream of Han-language Buddhism till today.

1. Tiantai Sect

Tiantai sect of Buddhism was founded by the patriarch Zhi Yi (538-597) during the Sui dynasty. His secular surname was Chen. Clever and apt at learning, he became a monk at the age of 18. At 23, he received his most important influences from his first teacher, Nanyue Hui Si (515-677), a meditation master who would later be listed as Zhi Yi's predecessor in the Tiantai lineage. After a period of study with Hui Si, he spent some time working in the southern capital of Jinling (567). Then he retired to Tiantai mountain for intensive study and practice of Lotus Sutra, because, to him, it was one of the most important Mahayana sutras preached by Sakyamuni. The Lotus Sutra is also known as Saddharmapundarika Sutra, or the Lotus of the Good Law, which was recognized for centuries by many Mahayana schools as containing the summit of Sakyamuni's teachings about supreme enlightenment and buddhahood. The Lotus Sutra describes the existence of an innate and universal truth, known as the Buddha nature, inherent in all life. It teaches profound respect for the dignity of life. The Lotus Sutra is unique among the teachings of Sakyamuni in that it affirms that the attainment of enlightenment is a possibility open to all people. That is the most influential teaching of Mahayana Buddhism or the Big Vehicle sect. It upgrades the supreme ideal of becoming an arhat (an enlightened saintly man) pursued by Hinayana Buddhism to the realm of becoming a Buddha. Mahayana and Hinayana are the two major factions of Buddhism. Mahayana was originated in India in the 1st century and was later introduced into China. By Mahayana, it means in Chinese the great conveyance or the greater vehicle, indicating that Buddhism believers may get enlightened and free from human sufferings by taking the vehicle. It describes primitive Buddhism and other sects later developed as Hinayana or lesser vehicle. Mahayana and Hinayana differ in many ways. Hinayana recognizes only one Buddha, that is, Sakyamuni while Mahayana is described as seeking to find and extend all knowledge, and, in certain schools, to lead all to Buddhahood. It has a conception of an Eternal Buddha. The theory supports the three realms of the past, present and future and the indefinite number of buddhas in the worlds in all directions: east, south, west, north, southwest, northeast, south east, northwest, upper level and lower level. But Hinayana is described to seek self-

◎ Guoqing Temple on Mount Tiantai, the patriarchal temple of Tiantai Sect.

attainment and self deliverance, with the highest goal of becoming Arhats.

Tiantai sect was very brisk during the Chi Yi period and reached its peak when it came to the seventh head of the Tiantai School Zhan Ran. Zhan Ran (711-782) evolved the theory that Buddha-nature remains in all things, even stones and grass. So he was regarded as upholding "pantheism". During the period of Emperor Wu Sect of the Tang dynasty (841-847), Buddhists were persecuted and Tiantai sect received a big blow. Yet the sect was introduced to the Korea Peninsula. Japanese monks also brought home the teachings of this sect. Till today, the Tiantai Buddhism is still exerting a big influence in Japan and the Republic of Korea. They take the Guoqing Temple on the Tiantai Mountain as the temple of its first patriarch and often send delegation to China to pay homage at Tiantai Mountain. Chinese monks of the Tiantai sect also often visit Tiantai temples in the Republic of Korea and Japan. In October 1985, a 19-member Japanese delegation of Tendai school of Buddhism visited Guoqing Temple of Tiantai Mountain. In 1987, Chinese Buddhist Association President Zhao Puchu headed a Chinese delegation to visit Enryakuji Temple. In 2001, a Chinese delegation headed by Chinese Buddhist Association Vice-President Diao Shuren and Guoqing Temple Abbot Master Ke Ming visited the Republic of Korea. The friendly exchanges among China, Japan and the Republic of Korea have never ceased.

2. Sanlun Sect

The Sanlun Sect or Madhyamika, was not originated in China. It was developed on the basis of such theories as "Madhyamika" or Nagarjuna's Twelve Gate Treatise, i.e. the Treatise in One Hundred Verses evolved by Indian monks Nagarjuna and Aryadeva. The three Buddhist scriptures mainly teach the idea of the nature void, i. e. the immateriality of the nature of all things, which belongs to the teaching of the Greater Vehicle Sect of Buddhism. Sanlun could not be counted as a sect in the early stage. The founder of the sect should be Kumarajiva (344-413). He was the most legendary figure in the history of Chinese Buddhism. There is a story about Kumarajiva in the "Biographies of Eminent Monks". According to the story, Kumarajiva (344-413 A.D.) was born in Kucha, in Central Asia. His father was Kumarajana, a Braham from India. He was kind and clever. When he was about to succeed his father as the prime minister of Kucha, he gave up and went into a mountain to become a monk. The King respected him and made him the master of the state. But

◎ Statue of Kumarajiva.

the King forced Kumarajana to marry his younger sister, who gave birth to Kumarajiva. Kumarajiva's mother was a wise woman, who could understand sutras being recited. She became a nun when Kumarajiva was seven years old. Kumarajiva followed his mother and learned Buddhist sutras. Like his mother, Kumarajiva could recite a thousand sutras/verses from memory. He won many debates organized by the King. At 12, he returned to Kucha. Many countries invited him to disseminate Buddhism and offered him high positions. But he refused. Later he met an arhat, who predicted that Kumarajiva would become a big Buddha. Kumarajiva became a fully ordained monk at the age of twenty, taking the precepts that Buddhist monks followed. Kumarajiva was well known in his country of Kucha and the neighboring countries. Later he invited his former teacher Bandhudatta to study Mahayana Buddhism. However, his mother encouraged Kumarajiva to carry the true teachings of Buddhism to China. Kumarajiva promised, despite his mother's warning that he would meet many troubles. When he lectured on Buddhism in the western areas, the kings of many states went to listen. In 385, Monarch Fu Jian of the Qin dynasty sent a cavalry to Kucha to snatch Kumarajiva, saying that he would not want the land and that he wanted to get Kumarajiva. During the battle, the King of Kucha was killed and Kumarajiva went with the Qin army. Kumarajiva arrived at Chang'an and was welcomed by King Yao Xing in 401. Kumarajiva was then over 50. King Yao Xing honored Kumarajiva with the title of National Preceptor, and asked him to take charge of the work of translating sutras into Chinese. King Yao Xing gathered more than 800 people including the then noted monks such as Hui Guan, Daosheng, Daorong and Sengzhao to re-translate Buddhist sutras.

Between 401-413 A.D. Kumarajiva translated 35 major sutras in 294 volumes. The most important among them were Astasahasrika Prajnaparamita Sutra i.e. the Perfection of Wisdom Sutra, Saddharmapundarika Sutra i.e. the Lotus Sutra, Vajracchedika Prajnaparamita Sutra i.e. the Diamond Sutra, Smaller Sukhavati-vguha, i.e. the Amitabha Sutra, Madhyamaka-shastra, i.e. the Treatise on the Middle, Shatika-shastra, i.e. the

Treatise in One Hundred Verses, Dvadashamukha Shastra i.e. the Treatise on the Twelve Gates, Sarvastivadin Vinaya i.e. the Ten-Category Vinaya , Satyasiddhi Shastra, i.e. Treatise on the Completion of Truth, Vimalakirti Nirdesha Sutra, i.e. Vimalakirti Sutra and Dasabhumikavibhasa.

Before Kumarajiva died, he proclaimed that if his translation was in accord with the genuine principles of Buddhism, his tongue would be intact and not turn to ash. After incineration of his body, the tongue was found to remain intact.

King Yao Xing quite appreciated Kumarajiva. He said that Kumarajiva was clever and superbly enlightened, unique in the world. In order to let him have offspring, he forced him to accept ten women and live a secular life. So although Kumarajiva had more than 3,000 students, no one made him teacher as he violated the commandments.

Two other persons were very important with regard to San Lun Sect. One is Kumarajiva's disciple Seng Zhao (384-414), who made important contributions to the building of the sect. The other is Ji Zang (549-623), who was regarded as the true founder of the San Lun Sect. Ji Zang, whose another name was Hu Jizang, was born in Jin Ling, with his ancestral home in what was known as Anxi State in western China. He began to study

San Lun or the three sutras at the age of 7 and was later invited by Emperor Tang of the Sui dynasty to the Riyan Temple in Chang'an (present-day Xi'an). He wrote the "Gist of Three Treatises", which became the main theories for the founding of the San Lun Sect, marking a new height in the theory of San Lun.

San Lun Sect emphasizes the notion of shunyata (emptiness) and wu (nonbeing), holding that loka (temporal world), supra-mundane, samskrta (active being), nirvana (non-active being) are all causally produced phenomena. So rigorous was the teaching of this lineage that it declared that the elements constituting perceived objects, when examined, are really no more than mental phenomena and have no true existence. Although the sect declined toward the end of the Tang dynasty, the Buddhist thought of maintaining the unreality of all things became the most important theories of the Greater Vehicle School of Buddhism and has remained till today.

The most famous temple of the first patriarch of San Lun sect is the Qixia Temple on the Qixia Hill on the outskirts of Nanjing in Jiangsu Province. It was built during the six dynasties period (483-489). Originally it was a private dwelling, with a temple in the back yard. Masters Seng Lang, Seng Quan and Fa

© Qixia Temple in Nanjing, Jiangsu Province.

Lang disseminated Buddhism in the temple. It was built and rebuilt several times from the Sui to Tang dynasties. In 1885, the fifth year of the reign of Emperor Xian Feng, the temple was burnt down by a fire and was later rebuilt again. Some 20 kilometers from downtown Nanjing City, it is a tranquil place. There is a vast open space in front of the front gate. Inside, there are the Hall of the Deva-kings, the Vairocana Hall, Assembly Hall, the Scripture Hall and the Hall in memory of Jian Zhen, a Buddhist master crossing the sea to disseminate Buddhism in Japan. A small door on the side of the last hall leads to a 15-meter high pagoda for Buddhist relics, originally built in the Sui Dynasty (581-618). It is an imitation made of wood with five stories. There are eight sides on each floor. At the base of the pagoda is a relief sculpture of the Buddha, while on the first floor are the sculptures of the four gods and flying apse. In the walls of 1,000-Buddhas Mountain Ridge, there are 294 niches, housing 515 Buddha statues. Nested deep in the bushes and hills, the temple enjoys a surrounding that is very beautiful, especially in the autumn when the whole mountain was covered with red leaves and the ancient temple, the 1000-Buddhas caves and the Buddhist relics pagoda hidden in the lush greens seem to make the mountain acquire soul.

3. Fa Xiang Sect

Fa Xiang sect or Dharmalaksana sect, was established in the 7th century after the return of Xuanzhang from India and his translation of the important Yogacarya works.

Xuan Zhuang contributed the most to the development of Buddhism in China and was a figure with an eminent status in the history of world culture.

Xuan Zhuang, whose secular surname was Chen, was born in 602 in Yanshi, Henan Province. His grandfather was a prominent scholar of the Northern Qi state and his father was a magistrate of Jiangling County. But his family was poor. Having been converted to Buddhism at an early age, he was fully ordained at the age of 21. When he was studying various sutras, he found many conflicting ideas and he decided to seek the original scriptures in Sanskrit. But his application to India in quest for Buddhist teachings was turned down by the imperial court. In 629, when a famine struck the country and the people fled their homeland to seek food, he mingled himself among the hungry people and left Chang'an on his way to India. He was then 26. He passed through Tianshui, Lanzhou and arrived at Liangzhou, where he was invited to expound Buddhist sutras. To overcome the language barrier, he learned Hindu from a man who knew the language. Then he arrived at Guazhou, a major town at the northwest border. A local official saw him off to Yumen Pass by providing him with some horses, cereals and daily use articles. Outside the Yumen Pass, there were five fire-signal platforms at a 100-li interval, guarded by Tang army. At the end of the last platform was a vast shifting sand river. The weather was capricious. Sometimes there were gale force winds; and sometimes there were lightening and thunder and rainstorms; sometimes, there was scorching sun. By sheer will, he crossed the river and came to the ancient state of Gaocang, which was an important city on the silk road. To the east was Dunhuang Grottoes and to the west was Kucha; Xuan Zhuang came to Kucha. There were many stone caves, which are the present-day 1000-Buddha caves. Another stone cave he passed through was the Kozer Stone cave in Xinjiang. Then, passing through a dozen smaller states, Xuanzuang came out of Congling to the southern part of the present-day Uzbekstan. In 630, Xuan Zhuang arrived in India after traveling for more than a year.

Xuan Zhuang visited Buddhagaya where Sakyamuni was born and Mahabodhi-sangharama, the monastery of the great enlightenment. At Rajagrha, he went into Nalanda Monastery, the highest Buddhist school in the then India to study Buddhism. First of all, he learned Yogacarabhumi-sastra from Silabhdra. Five years later, he visited dozens of small states. After returning to Nalanda Monastery, Silabhdra asked him to expound on Mahayana-samparigraha-sastra (collection of Mahayana treatises) and the treatise on the establishment of the doctrine on consciousness. He was also invited to participate in debates. Then, Rajaputra Saladitya invited him to speak on the doctrines of Mahayana at pancaparisad (quinquennual assembly) in Kanyakubja.

Xuan Zhuang returned to China in 645 after 17 years in quest of original Buddhist scriptures in Sanskrit, traveling 25,000 kilometers through 138 countries. He brought back 657 volumes of Buddhist scriptures. When arriving in Chang'an, he lived in the Hongfu Temple and then moved to Grand Ci'en Temple, immersing himself in translating the scriptures he brought back. He spent 20 years translating 75 Buddhist scriptures, totaling 1335 volumes, becoming one of four great translators in China.

Xuan Zhuang founded Fa Xiang sect, the first Buddhist

school in the Tang Dynasty. The
school mainly advocates for
three realms originating from the
mind and vijnanamatrasiddhi-
sastra (Treatise on the
establishment of the doctrine of
consciousness only). Xuan
Zhuang holds that all things are
originated in alaya-vijnana (the
storage consciousness) and all
the phenomena are derived from

◎ Portrait of Master Xuan Zhuang.

alaya-vijnana. The core theories of Fa Xiang sect are trilaksana
(three aspects of the nature of a thing) and alaya-vijnana. This
idea was not originated in India's Yogacara. Fa Xiang sect
maintains that the three planes of existence are merely the
manifestation of the conscious mind and that all phenomena are
the reflection of the sub -conscious mind. It also advocates for
eight perceptions (the eye, ear, nose, tong, body, consciousness,
non-consciousness and alaya-vijahana). It holds that all beings
possess Buddha-nature inherently, and thus all have the potential
for awakening and that one's potential for awakening was
determined by the good seeds already in one's consciousness

stream. Practitioners of the Hinayana, pratyekabuddha, and Mahayana paths, as well as those who were undecided about practice, could fulfill these paths only by bringing the respective seeds of whichever path they contained to fruition.

Fa Xiang sect recognizes Da Ci'en Temple and Xiangjiao Temple as temples of its first patriarch. Known as the best-preserved Buddhist temple complex, the Da Ci'en Temple was

initially built in the mid-7th century. It used to be a place where Xuan Zhuang translated Buddhist scriptures. Only 4 kilometers away from the Xi'an city proper, it was first built in the Sui Dynasty (581-618). At that time, it was named Wulou Temple. Later in AD 647 of the Tang Dynasty, Li Zhi (who became Emperor Tang

◎ Da Ci'en Temple in Xi'an, Shaanxi Province, the founding temple of Fa Xiang Sect.

◎ Xingjiao Temple, an important home of patriarchs of Fa Xiang Sect.

GaoSect in AD 649) ordered to rebuild this temple in memory of his late mother, Empress Wen De. It was a grand complex of building structures with a dozen courtyards and 2897 rooms and halls for monks. The temple subsequently gained its present name "Da Ci'en Temple".

In recent years, many halls of Tang style have been added, including the Memorial Hall for Xuan Zhuang. An inauguration ceremony was held in 2002 to mark the completion of the memorial hall.

The most important structure in the temple is what is known as the Big Goose Pagoda. It was a brick structure of five stories and about 60 meters (197 feet) high. The secular name, Big Goose, seems to have nothing to do with Buddhism. But there is a story behind this pagoda. According to historical records, the monks living in the Da Ci'en Temple had no meat to eat. They longed much for it so one of the monks started to pray to the God for blessing. At that very moment, a group of wild geese flew over the temple. Their heads dropped to the ground and they died. The monks were all surprised and thought it was the result of the Buddhist spirit so they decided to shun from eating meat forever.

Between AD 701 and AD 704, at the end of the reign of Empress Wu Zetian, five more stories were added to the original pagoda. But war at that time destroyed three stories, leaving seven. The current Big Goose Pagoda was rebuilt in the 17th century. It stands 64 meters, with each story having a brick arch cave, and the steps leading from the bottom to top. Although rebuilt time and again, the stone carving on "Buddha Preaching the Law" on both sides of the gate on the ground floor was the original of the Tang Dynasty. There is also a stone tablet in the niches on the eastern and western sides of the southern gate. It was said that they were put up by Xuan Zhuang himself. On the tablet on the eastern side is carved with the "Preface to the

Sanzhang Buddhism of Great Tang Dynasty". Inside the newly built memorial hall for Xuan Zhuang are exhibited the scalp bones of Xuan Zhuang. In 2003, Buddhists from all parts of the country visited the Da Ci'en Temple to attend a ceremony of the placement of Xuan Zhuang's bones.

Xingjiao Temple is also an important temple of the first patriarch of Fa Xiang sect. Situated in Anxian County, Shaanxi Province, it was built in 669 during the reign of Emperor Gao Sect of the Tang Dynasty. It was destroyed during the Qing Dynasty. The current structure was built in 1922-1934. Inside the temple, there is also a pagoda, built in 669. That is a place for placing the bones of Xuan Zhuang. Looking very much like the Big Goose Pagoda, it has five tiers, standing 23 meters. The pagoda was flanked by two 7-meter tall minor pagodas, one of Kuiji (632-682) and the other for Korean monk Wonchuk (613-696), both the close disciples of Xuan Zhuang.

4. Huayan Sect

The Huayan (Kegon) sect is named after the foundation work of Avatamsaka-sutra. It was said to be founded by Fazang or Xianshou Fazang, a name granted by Empress Wu Zetian. So this sect of Buddhism is also called Xianshou Sect or Xianshou Sect. Fazang was born to an official family in Samarkand or Soghdiana in today's Uzbekistan. His grandfather moved to Chang'an and his father was appointed as a prime minister. At the age of 17, he began to learn Avatamsaka-sutra from Zhiyan of the Fanghua Temple. Nine years later he was ordained as a monk. Fazang was well versed in Avatamsaka-sutra. Then Empress Wu Zetian ordered him to expound Avatamsaka-sutra in the temple and won the appreciation of the empress. During the reign of Emperior Zhong Sect of the Tang Dynasty, he got the permission to build Huayan temples in Chang'an, Luoyang and other places and serialized the theories of the Huayan Sect. But Dushun and Zhiyan were honored as the first and second patriarchs of Huayan Sect of Buddhism.

◎ Catang Temple, the founding temple of the Huayan Sect.

The core of Huayan teachings is the theory of interdependence of all things.

Huayan Sect takes Huayan Temple and Caotang Temple as the temples of the first patriarch.

Huayan Temple is in Chang'an County, Shaanxi Province. Built on a mountain slope in 803, it commands a beautiful landscape. It was destroyed during the Song Dynasty due to soil erosion, with only two pagodas left. One was built for the first patriarch Master Dushun. It stands 13 meters in seven stories, with the top story engraved with two Chinese words meaning "Master of Huayan". The other was built for the fourth patriarch

Qingliang Chengguan. It stands 7 meters in five stories and six sides.

Caotang Temple was originally the temple of the first patriarch of San Lun Sect. It is located in Huxian County, Shaanxi Province. It was a place where Kumarajiva translated Buddhist scriptures and his relic tower is still inside the temple. But the fifth Huayan patriarch Guifeng Sectmi lived in the temple. So it is also regarded as the temple of the first patriarch of Huayan Sect. There is a well in the temple, which gives out mists during autumn and winter, which has been regarded as a miracle. The temple is surrounded by steep ravines and grotesque peaks as well as water falls, looking very magnificent.

5. Lu Sect

Lu Sect or Lu Sect, which is also known as Vinaya, is a Buddhist school devoted to the study and maintenance of the rules and code of discipline of Buddhism. The Buddhist rules and disciplines or Vinaya were originated during the period of Sakyamuni when the assembly of monks necessitated the observation of common code of conduct.

In the 2nd-3rd centuries, all Chinese monks were not officially ordained. This situation was discovered by Dharmakala, an Indian monk, who came to Luoyang in 250 and prompted him to translate the rules and disciplines established with Buddhism. This book thus became the basis for Chinese monks for ordination. The theoretical founder of the Lu Sect was Hui Guang, who wrote "Commentaries on Dharmagupta-Vinaya". But the real founder was Dao Xuan (580-651). With his secular surname of Tie, Dao Xuan was born in Huzhou of Zhejiang Province. The legend has it that when his mother was pregnant, she dreamed of an Indian monk telling her that the embryo in her womb was the incarnation of a monk of Liang Dynasty and that she should let it be a monk after it was born. At the age of 15, he was bored by the secular life and took interest in Buddhism. One year later, he decided to learn Buddhism from Zhiyi and learned Vinaya disciplines from Zhishou. In 642, Dao Xuan moved into Fengde Temple on Zhongnan Mountain in Shaanxi. He founded the Vinaya altar in the mountains and established ceremonies for ordination and the Lu Sect or Vinaya Sect took shape.

The theories of the sect include commandments and rules,

◎ Daming Temple, the founding temple of the Lu Sect or Vinaya Buddhism.

embodiment of commandment, that is, the instinct of observing disciplines consciously after being ordained, behavior in compliance with the commandments, that is, the process of observing Vinaya

Chapter Two Han-Language Buddhism in China

◎ Statue of Monk Jian Zhen.

discipline, and the forms and contents of the Vinaya rules.

The Fengde Temple is no longer in existence. Dao Xuan's disciple Jian Zhen once spread teachings of Vinaya discipline in Daming Temple of Yangzhou and that temple has thus become the temple of the first patriarch of this sect of Buddhism.

Situated in a mountain on the northern outskirts of Yangzhou, the temple was built in the mid-5th century. The existing structure was built toward the end of the 19th century. The temple is noted as the residence of famous monk Jian Zhen, who was ordained in the temple at the age of 14 and became an abbot of the temple at the age of 27.

Inside the Daming Temple is a memorial hall for monk Jian Zhen. It was built in 1973 based on the design modeling on

◎ Jian Zhen Memorial Pavilion inside the Daming Temple.

Toshodai-ji of Japan by the most famous architect Liang Sicheng. Around the temple are many historical sites and a fountain known as the World's No. 5.

6. Mi Sect

Mi Sect, also known in Sanskrit as vajrayana, tantrayana or mantrayana, is the Mi Sect of the Tang Dynasty. It is so called relevant to open schools of Mahayana, different from Tantrism in Tibetan Buddhism. This sect professes to inherit Variocana. Variocana passed it on to Vajrasattva(-mahasattva), who, in turn, passed it on to Nagarjuna, then to Nagabodhi, Vajrobodhi and amoghavajra. But the real founders are three monks from India: Subhakasimha, Vajrabodhi and Amoghavajra.

Subhokarasimha (637-735), Indian pandit, had some relationship with Sakyamuni. Born into a royal family of Orissa, he inherited the throne at age of 13. But his brothers began a violent struggle over the succession. He was wounded by an arrow but put down the rebellion. He pardoned his brothers and renounced the throne and became a Buddhist monk, settling in Venuvanavihara at Nalanda monastery. At the behest of his master Dharmagupta, he embarked on a journey to holy places of Sakyamuni. He traveled to many countries and everywhere he went he had wild animals as his guide and in every cave where he lived, there were portraits of Sakyamuni. In 716, he came to China. He was met by Emperor Xuan Zong and began translating Buddhist texts. In the 12th year of Emperor Kai Yuan, he moved to a temple in Luoyang, continuing his translation work.

Vajrabodhi (669-741),a Malayan of Southern India, translated into Chinese as State of Guangming. His father was Brahman. As an infant, Vajrabodhi could recite scriptures and firmly committed to memory. He became a monk at the age of 16 and went to Nalanda Monastery to study Buddhist teachings. Ten years later, he became well versed in Tripitaka. When he heard that Buddhism was flourishing in China, he set sail to China. He spent several years on the seas, experiencing untold sufferings and arrived in Guangzhou, China, in 719 and then in Luoyang a year later. At first, he lived in Ci'en Temple and later moved to Dajianfu Temple. Everywhere he went, he built Mandala altar for consecrating his disciples by pouring water on the head. In Dajianfu Temple he led his disciples in translating Buddhist scriptures, making Mi Sect flourish in Luoyang and Chang'an and spread to other parts of the country.

Amoghavajra (705-774) or Bukong in Chinese, was born in a Brahman family in northern India. Both his parents died when he was young. He came to China with his uncle at the age of 10. At 15, he was ordained into the sangha by Vajrabodhi and became his disciple. As he knew many languages, Vajrabodhi asked him to translate Buddhist scriptures. Three years later, he wanted to return to India and Vajrabodhi taught him five more Buddhist scriptures. Then he left China and went on a pilgrimage to gather texts, visiting Sri Lanka, Southeast Asia and India. In Sri Lanka, he was invited to the court and the King washed him with fragrant water contained in a gold kettle. He then taught the court Buddhist teachings and built altars for preaching. He returned to China in 746 with some five hundred volumes of scriptures. The Chinese emperor asked him to live in Honglu Temple and later he was summoned to the imperial court to initiate Emperor Xuan Zong by pouring water on his head. The emperor granted his Buddhist name Zhi Zang. He received even more respect when Emperor Dai Zong ascended the throne. During this period, he translated a number of sutras, including the Tattvasamgraha and sutra of the benevolent King. The emperor wrote the preface to the sutras and promulgated them. On the day when the sutras were issued, auspicious clouds swept across the land and the whole country celebrated. Later, when the emperor summoned Amoghavajra to Wutai Mountain to preach Buddhism, a comet appeared in the sky. After the service was over, the comet disappeared. In 771, when the emperor celebrated his birthday anniversary, Amoghavajra presented him with 77 sutras in 120 volumes as birthday present. Before his death, he left to the emperor the vajra and silver plates and other valuable things passed on to him by Vajrabodhi. On June 15 of the year, Amoghavajra washed himself in fragrant water, lied down in his bed, with head toward the east and face toward the imperial court, quietly passing away.

The Mi Sect of the Tang Dynasty was founded on Mahavairocana-Sutra and Vajrasekhara-Sutra. The way is very complicated to learn, as it has to be passed on in person by Mi Sect masters in special services. It has an aura of mystery over it. The Mi Sect of the Tang Dynasty was passed on to Huiguo, a disciple of Amoghavajra, before it was interrupted. But disciple of Huiguo, Japanese monk Kukai, brought the teachings of the sect to Japan, which was later developed into Shingon-shu.

The temples of the first patriarch of the Mi Sect of Buddhism in the Tang Dynasty are Daxingshan Temple and Qinglong Temple in Xi'an, Shaanxi Province. It was built in 582, the second year of the first emperor of the Sui Dynasty. When Emperor Wen ascended the throne, he built the first state scripture translation center. It remained one of the three major translation centers till the Tang dynasty. The translation work in Daxingshan Temple occupied an important position in the whole scripture translation in the Sui Dynasty. Toward the end of the Sui Dynasty and at the beginning of the Tang period, Chinese Buddhism met great setbacks and the translation work stopped. The work did not resume until 629 then Tang Emperor Tai Zong summoned Indian monk Bodun to reopen the translation center.

Daxingshan Temple was a place where Amoghavajra passed on the teachings of the Mi Sect and held initiation ceremonies, thus founding Mi Sect. The temple was destroyed on several occasions. Major repairs and rebuilding started in the winter of 1955 only to be damaged during the Cultural Revolution (1966-1976). The current structure has five courtyards, including a main entrance gate, the Heavenly King Hall, the Drum and Bell Tower, the Hall of Mahavira and the Hall of Avalokitesvara.

The Qinglong Temple is located in the southern suburbs of Xi'an City. Built in 582, it served as a site for holding consecration ceremony, hence becoming a temple of the first patriarch of Mi Sect. Japanese monk Kukai once learned Mi Sect in the place and so it is also upheld as the ancestral hall of Japanese Shingon-shu. In the 1990s, two memorial halls were built on the ruins of the Tang temple, one for Japanese monk Kukai and the other for

Huiguo. The Qinglong Temple stands witness to the friendly exchanges of Chinese and Japanese Buddhists.

7. Jingtu Sect

Jingtu Sect or Pure Land Sect is a branch school of Buddhism that teaches relatively simple methods of recitation of the Buddha's name for the purpose of attaining rebirth in the Western Heaven (Pure Land). It holds that there is a paradise in the Western World, with the master being Amitabha. It was first founded in the Eastern Jin Dynasty by Hui Yuan (334-416). But in fact, the founder was Shandao (613-681) of the Tang Dynasty.

Shandao was born in Linzi (present-day Zibo of Shandong Province). He learned "Lotus Sutra" and "Vimalakirtinirdesa-sutra". He went to the Xuanzhong Temple in Shanxi Province in 641 during the Tang Emperor Tai Zong period, then to Guangming Temple in Xi'an. He is said to have copied the Amitabha-sutra more than 100,000 times and made more than 300 paintings of the Pure Land. He was regarded as the incarnation of Amitabha. Legend has it that his mouth was shining with Buddhist light when he was repeating the name of Amitabha and that was why Emperor Gao Zong changed the name of the residence of Shandao into "Guangming Temple". He wrote five works in nine fascicles, including commentaries on different sections of the "Sutra of Meditation on the Buddha of Infinite Life".

Donglin Temple was the birthplace of the Pure Land Sect of Buddhism, Located on Mount Lushan in Jiangxi Province, it commands a beautiful landscape, with a stream flowing through it year round. It was first built in the Eastern Jin dynasty and was repaired and rebuilt on many occasions over the past century. During the Tang Dynasty, it had 310 halls and rooms and was one of the temples that stored the most Buddhist texts. It was rebuilt twice in the Ming Dynasty and twice in the Qing Dynasty. It is only in recent years that the temple has been restored.

Donglin Temple was a service site founded by Hui Yuan, the first patriarch of the Pure Land Sect. Hui Yuan, whose secular surname was Jia, was a native of Ningwu of Shanxi Province. He was born in 334. He studied Confucianism and Daoism when a child. When he became a monk, he learned Buddhism from Dao'an and became his disciple. When wars broke out in northern China, he followed Dao'an down to the south, first to Xiangyang and then to Jingzhou. In 381, he came to Lushan and built a garden there. In 386, the garden was turned into a temple. As it was located east of the Xilin Temple, it was named Donglin Temple. Since then, he made Donglin Temple a center for spreading the teachings of the Pure Land Sect. As at that time, Buddhism introduced from India was not infused with the local culture, Hui Yuan integrated Buddhism with Confucianism and Daoism and that won the support of the ruler and was favored by the common people. He also invited Liu Yimin and Zhou Xuzhi and other famous monks to dig ponds to plant lotus flowers and set up the "White Lotus Society". That is why the Pure Land Sect is also known as "Lian Sect" (Lotus Sect). Hui Yuan was held up as the first patriarch of the sect. There is still a lotus pond in the temple.

There are many historical sites near Donglin Temple. The hills, water, spring and stones as well as building structures are all associated with Buddhism and stories about the meritorious deeds of Hui Yuan. In the eastern side of the temple, there is a big pine tree and by it was a tablet in which the words "Pine for Six Dynasties" are engraved. It is said that the tree was planted by Hui Yuan in person.

On the hill behind the Donglin Temple, there is an upper pagoda. It is said that five pieces of the bones of the Buddha brought back by Buddhabhadra (359-429) are kept there. Down

◎ Xuanzhong Temple in Shanxi.

the hill, there is a lower pagoda or Yanmen pagoda as it is called. It is the burial place of Hui Yuan. It was repaired in 1984.

The structures of the Donglin temple were mostly built after the 1966-1976 Cultural Revolution.

Xuanzhong Temple, also known as Yongningchan Temple, is located deep in the Shibi Mountain in Jiaocheng County, Shanxi Province. It used to be a service site of the Pure Land Sect founded by Master Tan Luan of the northern Wei Dynasty and is also the common temple of the first patriarch of Chinese Pure Land Sect and Japanese Shingo-shu.

Work to build the temple started in 472 and was completed in 476. In 609, Dao Zuo moved into the temple. Emperor Tai

Zong, li Shimin, visited Taiyuan and made a special trip to pay homage to Dao Cuo in 635. In 641, Master Shandao came to the temple and became a disciple of Dao Cuo. After the death of Dao Cuo, Shandao left the temple for Guangming Temple.

The main hall of the temple was burned down during the years of Emperor Guang Xu of the Qing Dynasty. Since then, it was left in disrepairs and abandoned. In 1937, the temple was robbed and thrown into even worse plight. There was only the Tianwang Hall and some dilapidated rooms for monks were left in 1949. After 1954, the Chinese cultural relics department appropriated money on six occasions for repairing and rebuilding the temple.

Preserved in the temple are tablets of the northern Wei, Northern Qi (564), Tang and Yuan dynasties.

Xuanzhong Temple has

◎ Statue of Shandao presented to Xuanzhong Temple by Japanese Jodo-shu.

close relationship with Japanese Jodo-shu, which was founded in 1175 by Honen on the basis of Shandao's "Guan Wu Liang Shou Fo Jingshu" (Commentray on Amitayurdhyana Sutra). His disciple Shinran founded the Jodo-shin or shin sect.

The Japanese Jogo-shu sect regards Xuanzhong Temple as the temple of its first patriarch. There are Japanese Buddhists visiting the temple every year. A monk of Zojo-ji in Tokyo moved a date tree from the temple and transplanted it in Zoho-ji and renamed the temple Date Temple. When the Abbot died in 1982, his disciples buried part of the ashes in the Xuanzhong Temple according to the will left by the senior monk.

8. *Chan Sect*

Chan Sect or meditation school of Buddhism was originated in Sakyamuni and has become a Buddhist sect with distinct Chinese features.

According to Buddhist scriptures, this sect, believing in direct enlightenment, disregards ritual and sutras and depends upon the inner light and personal influence for the propagation of its tenets. It was founded on the esoteric tradition supposed to have been imparted to Kasyapa by the Buddha, who indicated his meaning by plucking a flower without further explanation. Kasyapa smiled in apprehension and is supposed to have passed on this mystic method to the patriarchs. So Kasyapa became the first patriarch of this dharmaparyaya, a doctrine, or wisdom of the Buddha regarded as the door to enlightenment. After Kasyapa, dharmaparyaya was passed on for 27 generations in India and Bodhidharma, ostensibly the twenty-eighth patriarch in a lineage. Bodhidharma is said to arrive in Guangzhou, bringing with him dharmaparyaya, a way teaching a "separate transmission outside of the texts" which "did not rely upon textuality." Then he founded Chan Sect and Bodhidharma became the first patriarch.

In 527, Bodhidharma came to Shaolin Temple in Songshan. Legend has it that he spent nine years in meditation, facing the rock wall of a cave about a mile from the Shaolin Temple. That is a special way of meditation created by Bodhidharma, with the purpose of achieving the original essence of Buddhist practice - meditation and the cultivation of the right view. It was said that because Bodhidharma spent nine years in the cave, his shadow was imprinted on the rock wall and by and by it cannot be erased.

Bodhidharma died in 528, said to be poisoned in Luoshui River or die in meditation. After his death, Emperor Dai Zong of the Tang Dynasty granted the name "Master of Perfect Enlightenment" to him.

Huineng (638-713), with the secular surname of Lu, had his ancestral home in Fanyang of Hebei Province (present-day Zuoxian County, Hebei Province) but was born in Xinzhou (present-day Xinxing County, Guangdong Province). He bereft of his father when young. He had to provide for his mother and himself by gathering firewood and selling it in the marketplace. It was at one of these marketplaces that he heard a verse from the Diamond Sutra -- "Let your mind flow freely without dwelling on anything" -- that illumined his mind and set his soul afire. When Huineng first came to the monastery of the Fifth Patriarch, Hongren, he was an unimpressive figure - a poor boy from the backward countryside who did not even know how to read or write. The learned monks at the monastery paid him to heed and in

◎ Statue of the sixth patriarch Huineng of the Chan Sect.

general considered him beneath contempt. When asked what he could do, he replied that he could work the mill. Patriarch Hongren arranged a job for him in the mill house. Eight months later, when the time came for the Fifth Patriarch to name his successor, he ordered all the disciples to express their understanding of the Chan Buddhist teachings in whatever way they saw fit. The one who could demonstrate the utmost understanding would become the next Patriarch.

The most learned disciple at the monastery was the head

monk Shenxiu, who was an accomplished scholar. Most monks felt certain that the mantle would go to him, and there was no his match among others for Shenxiu's intellects.

To demonstrate his wisdom, Shenxiu wrote his famous poem:

> The body is the bodhi tree
> The heart is like the clear mirror stand
> At all times diligently wipe it clean
> Do not let it attract dust

Huineng understood instantly where Shenxiu fell short. There was another level of wisdom beyond that described in Shenxiu's poem. Huineng knew how to express this understanding in a poem - but being illiterate, did not know how to write it down. He ended up asking another monk to write it up on the same wall for him:

> Bodhi really has no tree
> Nor is clear mirror the stand
> Nothing's there initially
> So where can the dust motes land?

When they saw this poetic response, the monks did not get it at all. But the Fifth Patriarch comprehended Huineng's meaning perfectly. Represented in these four lines was an intuitive mind more capable of grasping fundamental concepts than Shenxiu's formidable intellect after decades of schooling.

Now, if the Fifth Patriarch were to announce Huineng's succession publicly and hand the reins over to him, he knew that the monks would not understand. They probably would turn on Huineng and possibly even cause him harm just to prevent him from assuming the office. Therefore, he pretended to be unimpressed with the response. In great secrecy, and in the middle of the night, he passed the symbol of his authority - a bowl and a robe - to Huineng.

Chan has its basis in the conviction that the world and its components are one reality. Reason, by analyzing the diversity of the world, obscures this oneness. Enlightenment about the nature of reality can be apprehended by the non-rational part of the mind --the intuition-- through meditation. Huineng's central insight is in pointing out the transient or "illusory" nature of the physical world. He got the essence of Buddhism and that was why Hongren picked him as successor. But picking successor was an extremely important event and competition was very fierce, even at the price of life. So in great secrecy, and in the middle of the night, he passed the symbol of his authority - a bowl and a robe - to Huineng and ordered him to flee for his life. Huineng did hastily depart the monastery, with a mob of angry monks in hot pursuit. He did not appear until more than 10 years later when he came upon a monastery known as Faxing Temple in Guangzhou (present-day Guangxiao Temple) in which its Master was speaking on the Mahaparinirvana Sutra. Two monks who were listening were locked in a dispute over whether the fluttering motion of the pataka outside the temple was caused by wind or by itself. Intrigued, he stayed to listen and chimed in, saying: "It is driven neither by the wind nor by itself. It is your hearts that are beating." The dharma master was impressed, recognized him as a dharma-successor, and invited him to join them and be initiated in their Order. The following year, Huineng returned to Baolin Temple (now Nanhua Temple) and lived there, spreading Buddhism, for more than 30 years. His disciple Fahai sorted out his teachings and compiled into "Analects of the Sixth Chan Patriarch Huineng". Huineng had many disciples. Most prominent among them were Qingyuan, Nanyue and Heze, who later developed their own schools of thought.

The temple of the first patriarch of Chan Sect is Shaolin

Temple at the foot of the Songshan Mountain in Dengfeng county, Henan province. It is known as the "No. 1 Temple under Heaven". Built in 495, Bodhidharma passed on the teachings of Chan Buddhism. The fact that Shaolin Temple is known far and wide in the world not because it is the temple of the first patriarch of Chan Buddhism, but because of its Wushu or Kungfu. In recent years, monks of the Shaolin Temple have been to many countries

◎ Shaolin Temple, the founding temple for the Chan Sect.

in the world to perform Wushu or Kungfu. When in Britain, they were granted audience by Queen Elizabeth. The Shaolin Temple was destroyed many times in history. The latest was in 1928 when Warlord Shi Yousan set fire on it and the fire lasted five days and nights. After the founding of the People's Republic, it has been rebuilt and repaired on many occasions. The current complex is much larger than ordinary temples, but as compared with what it was in ancient times, it still looks a little smaller. In it are many stone tablets handed down from ancient times. The most prominent is the plaque of the temple, which was in the hand of Emperor of the Qing Dynasty. At the northern end of the Shaolin Temple, there is a 1000-Buddha Hall, which is the biggest hall in the Shaolin Temple. Inside are the portraits of Vairocana, Amitabha and Bodhidharma. On the northern, eastern and western walls are murals of more than 500 years ago, depicting 500 arhats paying homage to Vairocana. The whole picture measures more than 300 square meters. In the hall are many pit holes, said to be caused by monks when exercising Kungfu. Close to the temple are the convents of the first and second patriarchs of Chan Buddhism and Cave of Bodhidharma.

Another temple of the founders of Chan Buddhism is the Nanhua Temple on the outskirts of Shaoguan, Guangdong

◎ Lingzhao Pagoda at Nanhua Temple.

Province. It is noted for its peaks and streams and beautiful landscape that surrounds it. Built in 677, the sixth patriarch of the Chan Sect Huineng preached Chan tenets there. There is a Sixth Patriarch Hall for the flesh body portrait Huineng when he died sitting. It is said that some highly enlightened senior monks does not only know the exact time of his death but also dies there sitting. The flesh body portrait of Huineng remained intact for the last 1000 years. Inside the temple, there was also a spring found in the 7th century, the Lingzhao Pagoda of the 10th century and wooden sculpture of 500 arhats.

Of the eight sects of Buddhism in China, only the Chan and Pure Land schools have maintained their vitality and the rest have had little influence. But research into these sects of Buddhism has never stopped.

9. Four famous mountains associated with Han-Language Buddhism

The temples of Han-Language Buddhism are mostly built on famous mountains and scenic spots. The most famous among them are Wutai, Putuo, Jiuhua and E'mei.

MOUNT WUTAI

Mount Wutai is located deep in the mountains in Wutai County in Shanxi Province, about 120 kilometers north of the city of Taiyuan. It is so named because it consists of five platform-shaped peaks. All the five peaks are more than 2,500 meters above sea level, with the highest at 3,058 meters above sea level. The weather there is cold and the denuded peaks are covered by snow all year round, though the slopes are thickly forested, presenting a typical scene of North China.

Surrounded by the five mountain peaks are densely distributed temples, with the Town of Taihuai at the center. When Buddhism enjoyed its golden period, there were more than 300 temples. Even now, there are more than 100 left. All the temples have been rebuilt or repaired over the past two decades.

As Mount Wutai is the bodhimandala of Manjusri (bodhisattva of Wisdom), the temples mainly worship Manjusri.

Xiantong Temple (Prominence Temple) is one of the most famous. Built more than 1,600 years ago during the reign of Emperor Ming of the eastern Hay Dynasty, the temple boasts a giant bell, weighing about 5,000 kilograms, the biggest in Mount Wutai. There are also many other structures unique in style, including the Amitayus Hall, a magnificent brick structure without a single beam, and the Bronze Hall 8.3 meters high, 4.7

◎ Stone memorial gateway to Longquan Temple on Mount Wutai.

◎ First snow on Mount Wutai.

meters wide and 4.5 meters in depth, with the walls on the four sides carved with Buddhist and animal images.

Down below the Xiantong Temple is the Tayuan Temple, in which there is a big white pagoda standing 50 meters, with 250 bells hung in the waist and top of the pagoda, jingling pleasantly in the breeze. The pagoda is regarded as a signature structure of Mount Wutai, which has become a main subject for paintings and photographic works. Behind the pagoda is the Lingjiu Mountain and the sky-piercing Pusading Temple (Buddha's Peak Temple) leading down the mountain by 108 flights of stairs. It used to be a place of pilgrimage for some famous Buddhist monks and even emperors.

MOUNT PUTUO

Mount Putuo is a narrow strip isle in the Zhoushan Archipelago. It used to be the service site of bodhimandala of Bodhisattva Avalokitesvara, the Goddess of Mercy.

Located 5 km east of the Zhoushan Islands off the coast of Zhejiang Province, temple was built with the elevation of the mountain overhanging with cliffs and proliferating bamboo bushes. The temple complex includes Puji Temple, Fayu Temple and Huiji Temple. The Puji Temple is closest to the sea. In front

◎ Chaoyin Cave (Tidal Wave Sound Cave) on Mount Putuo.

◎　Outdoor statue of Bodhisattva Avalokitesvara on Mount Putuo.

音 觀 海 南

of it is a lotus flower pond, also known as Fangsheng Pond or pond for monks to release fish. There is a smaller isle east of the Putuo Mountain, measuring less than one square kilometer in area. Legend has it that Bodhisattva Avalokitesvara meditated there. In ordinary times, there are only a few people crossing the sea to the Isle by small boats. At night, only spots of lights can be seen. Mount Putuo is not only a sacred place of Buddhism but also a fascinating beautiful scenic zone. It has many grotesque scenic spots. Among them is the Chaoyin Cave. It is a Buddhist hall built on a breathtaking cliff. Below it is the surging waves of the sea. When water tumbles into the cave and bumps into the rocks inside, it produces thunderous roars. Buddhists often compare their sounds of recitation of Buddhist scriptures to the roaring sea waves. Listening to the roaring sound in the cave, the Buddhists are as if hearing the preaching of the Buddha that purifies their soul and imparting enlightenment.

MOUNT JIUHUA

Mount Jiuhua, a place where Ksitigarbha held services, is located in the Qingyang County, Anhui Province. To the north is the Yangtze River and to the west is Mount Huang. The mountain has 99 peaks, with Shiwang as the highest, standing 1342 meters above sea level. Mount Jiuhua is full of waterfalls, streams, exotic-looking boulders, ancient caves, old pines and exuberant bamboo. The ancient temples are tucked in the dense woods. There were more than 300 temples during the peak period in

◎ Ganlu Temple on Mount Jiuhua.

history. Existing now are more than 80. Among them are Huacheng, the Hall of Sacred Remains, the Hall of Longevity and Ganlu. The Hall of the Sacred Remains was a place where Kim Gio Gak, scion of the imperial family of one of the three Korean Kingdoms died and buried. Inside the temple is a red wooden tower standing seven stories with eight sides, where the remains of the Korean Ksitigarbha Kim are displayed.

On top of the mountain, there is the Hall of Longevity. Inside it, there is the sculpture of an old monk who died at the age of 126. It is said that he lived in the mountains alone, just eating medicinal herbs and drinking mountain spring water. He was

◎ Zhiyuan Temple on Mount Jiuhua.

found three years after his death. He was later held up as a flawless Buddha.

One of the mysteries with Mount Jiuhua is that after the death of a monk, the remains stays perfectly well without any anti-septic treatment.

MOUNT EMEI

Mount Emei, the bodhimandala of Samantabhadra, God of Universal Benevolence and disciple of Sakyamuni, rises 3,099 meters above the sea level in Emei County, 160 kilometers southwest of Chengdu. It has three main peaks: Da'e, er'e and San'e, with Da'e being the tallest. From a distance, the Da'e and Er'e mountains look like a pair of brows that extend long, slender and curved in a picturesque fashion, just like the delicate eyebrows of a beautiful woman, hence the name of the mountain Emei which literally means "delicate eyebrows". Emei is noted for its rains, mists and clouds. There are more than 50 big and small temples and the most famous among them are: Baoguo (Devotion to the Country), Wannian (Ten-Thousand-Year), Xixiang (Elephant Bath) and Leiyin (Sound of Thunder). A bronze statue of Samantabhadra is found in every temple there.

The Baoguo Temple leans against the mountain, rising with

the mountain terrain. It boasts three treasures: a 12.5-ton bronze bell, a 500-year-old porcelain statue of the Buddha and a 10-storeyed bronze Huayan Pagoda, standing 7 meters, with 4,700 small Buddhist images carved on it and a complete text of Huayan Sutra or Garland Sutra or Buddhavatamsaka-mahavaipulya sutra in Sanskrit.

◎ The statue of Samantabhadra riding his white elephant in the Wannian Temple (Longevity Temple).

The Wannian or the Longevity Temple is the most famous and the biggest temple on Mount Emei. It is said that the temple was built in 399 by Monk Huite and the first emperor of the Song dynasty presented Buddhist scripture, monk's gown and a treasure ring to the temple. He also granted 3,000 ounces of gold to buy bronze for building a statue of Samantabhadra riding his white elephant. The statue stands 7.35-meter high and weighs 62 tons. The statue is now in

◎ Beamless brick-structured hall of the Wannian Temple.

a beamless hall of brick structure featuring a blended style of Myanmar and India. Around the statue are 3,000 Buddhist images and 500 images of arhats. In front of the temple, there is a water pond. In it are many frogs. When the frogs sing, they produce a sound like that of Chinese violin.

CHAPTER THREE
TIBETAN BUDDHISM IN CHINA

1. Origin and Development of Tibetan Language Buddhism

Tibetan language Buddhism or simply Tibetan Buddhism was originated in the 7th century when Buddhism was introduced into China. But it did not take shape after a long period of interaction and struggle with the local Bon religion. Tibetan Buddhism mainly spread among Tibetans and Mongolians in Tibet and Qinghai. Virtually all Tibetans and Mongolians are Buddhists. There are also a significant portion of Yugu, Menba, Luoba, Tu and Qiang people of minority nationalities believing in Buddhism. Now, Tibetan Buddhism has made itself increasingly felt in the world, spreading to many parts of the world, such as India, Nepal, the People's Republic of Mongolia, Bhutan, Sikkim and Russia and even in European and North American countries. At the beginning of the Founding of the People's Republic of China, there were more than 5,000 Tibetan Buddhist monasteries, with more than 400,000 monks. The number dropped drastically during the 1966-1967 Cultural Revolution period and it did not rise until the 1980s.

It is said that Buddhism was introduced into Tibet during the Tubo Kingdom period in about the 4th century. One day, the Tubo King suddenly found several mysterious objects falling from the sky, which were "Confession Sutra", a golden Buddhist Relics tower and "Six-Word Charm" (Om, Mani, Madme, Hum) and mysterious written language. There was no written language in the locality at the time and there was no way of recognizing alien languages. According to historical documents, these objects were brought to Tibet by Indians Buddhists. Upon seeing that Tibetans had no idea of their significance, the Indian monks had no choice but to secret them in a safe place and return to India. The fact remains that Buddhism did spread into Tibet during the reign of Tubo King Songtsan Gambo (629-650) in the 7th century.

At the time, Tibet was surrounded by Buddhist countries

such as India and Nepal in the South, the Tang Dynasty in the east. Songtsan Gambo did his best to establish friendly ties with neighboring countries. He married Princess Khridzun of Nepal and Princess Wencheng of the Tang Dynasty (618-907). Each princess journeyed to Tibet with the statue of the Buddha and the images of Meitreya and Sgrol-ma and once there set about building the Jokhang and Ramoge monasteries in Lhasa. All the monasteries have the statues of Sakyamuni, Meitreya, Avalokitesvara and Sgrol-ma. Translation of Buddhist texts also began under the direction of the Han monk Da Tian Shou.

Buddhism did not develop further during the two generations of Gambos after King Songtsan Gambo, because the force of the local Bon religion was too strong to resist. Buddhism failed to flourish until Tride Zhotsan, great grandson of Songtsan Gambo, finally took power. In 710, Tride Zhotsan asked for the hand of and eventually married Princess Jincheng of the Tang Dynasty. The new bride moved the statue of Buddha, which Princess Wencheng brought to Tibet, to the Jokhang Monastery. Meanwhile, she arranged monks accompanying her to the Tubo Kingdom to take charge of the monastery and related religious activities. Besides, wars and persecution of monks in some Buddhist countries in the Western Regions drove a massive

◎ Statue of Sakyamuni brought into Tibet by Princess Wencheng.

number of monks to Tubo. This again sparked discontent amongst ministers worshipping the Bon religion. The ministers left no stone unturned to obstruct the development of Buddhism. The situation lasted until Trisong Detsan, the son of Tride Zhotsan, came to power. Trison Detsan relied on Buddhism to fight ministers who rallied behind the Bon religion. As part of the effort, he invited Santaraksita from Nepal and famous Indian monk Padmasambhava, who were believed to be able to conquer all evils. Padmasambhava waged a tenacious struggle against Bon followers. The fiercest fight took place when he was leading artisans in building the Samye Monastery in 799. The monastery, which was modeled on the ideal world "Great Bhiliocosm", was completed in the late 8th century, with the lower storey in the Tibetan style, middle storey in the Han style and the upper storey in the Indian style. It is not only the earliest monastery for both the secret and open sects of Buddhism but also the earliest to have its independent property. Seven noble children were later tonsured to the monastery, which became the first monastery in Tibetan Buddhist history to tonsure monks. The event thus pioneered the tonsure system of Tibetan Buddhism. Later the seven tonsured children were held up as "Seven Enlightened Ones", each with a name associated with Santaraksita. This is a major event in the history of Tibetan Buddhism.

After Trison Detsan died in 797, his son Moni Gampo came to power. But later he was poisoned to death by his mother for his vigorous efforts to develop Buddhism. Then his younger brother Sainalay ascended the throne. He continued the efforts to develop Buddhism and fought against anti-Buddhism forces. After his death, his fifth son Reba came to power. But he was also killed during the fierce conflict in the palace between the two conflicting factions. The ministers threw their support behind the anti-Buddhist Darma. King Glan Darma launched a large scaled suppression of Buddhists, closing down monasteries, destroying Buddhist images and statues, defacing murals, set Buddhist scriptures on fire and persecuting monks. The anti-Buddhist activities lasted for more than 100 years. This is known as "Buddhism Suppression Period" that ended the 200-year earlier stage of Buddhism in Tibet.

In 842, King Glan Darma was killed by a Buddhist monk known as Beiji Doji. Most monks fled, some to the Ngari area, some to Dokang area and some to Xinjiang and Qinghai. Buddhism did not revive until the 1070s, when the fleeing monks sent disciples to Amdo area to learn Buddhist teachings and when they returned, they built monasteries and expanded the ranks of monks. The Tibetan King in the Ngari region invited Anagarika Dharmapala and others from Nepal and other places to the region to spread Buddhism. This is a period known as the "latter stage of the propagation of Tibetan Buddhism". During this period, translation of Buddhist scriptures also picked up speed. The

Buddhist converted Tibetan King Yesho when spreading Buddhism in Ngari region and found that the Tantrism was neither authentic nor complete and there were even places that violated the teachings of Buddhism. He then sent 21 monks to India to learn authentic Buddhism. Reqen Sampo and Lekbe Sherap returned and engaged in the translation of Buddhist scriptures. After that, many Indian Monks came to Tibet and boosted the development of the Tantric Buddhism. During the more than 300 years from the end of the 10th century to the 13th century, Tibet and India never stopped exchanging of monks. That led to the formation of various sects of Buddhism in Tibet.

2. Major Sects of Tibetan Buddhism

NYINGMA SECT

Nyingmapa, meaning the Ancient Ones, dates from around 750 with Padmambhava. As its name suggests, it is the oldest of the Buddhist sects in Tibet. The formation of this sect was accredited to three persons of the Zur family, namely, Zur Poche, Zur Chung Shesrap Dragpa, Zur Chung Sgro-phug-pa, the followers of Indian monk Padmasambhava, also known as Guru Rinpoche, who came to Tibet in 817. The Nyingmapa lamas wear red robes and hats, so it is also known as the Red Sect. It has a loose organization and focuses on mantra practice.

Its fundamentals are 18 Tantras. But only eight are the most practised. The first five are on the ways of appearing in the world and the other three are about the ways of leaving the world. The main practices are emphasized in the three inner Tantras of Maha Yoga, Anu Yoga, and Ati Yoga. Ati Yoga is also known as the Great Perfection, Dzogpa Chenpo, or simply as Dzogchen. The practice of Dzogchen is the heart of the Nyingma tradition.

Nyingmapa lamas believe that the mind is pure and that only by cultivating one's being in such a way as to reject all outside influences, is it possible to become as one with Buddha.

The Nyingma lineage identifies three specific lines of transmission of the Vajrayana teachings of the tantras: Kama, or the oral transmission lineage of the Buddha; Terma, or the revealed treasure lineage; and Daknang or visionary or the human ear-whispered lineage.

Guru Rinpoche was a Vajrayana master, and he taught widely from the highest classes of tantra, the textual vehicles of the Vajrayana. In particular, he transmitted these Vajrayana teachings to his twenty-five principal disciples. These first Tibetan masters became renowned for their spiritual accomplishments. The continuous, unbroken transmission from Guru Rinpoche through these principal disciples to their own disciples and so forth is called Kama, the oral transmission lineage.

Padmasambhava also hid hundreds of scriptures, images and ritual articles throughout Tibet. These items became known as "Treasures," and were concealed in many different ways. At the same time, Padmasambhava left precise instructions on how to discover and reveal these treasures for the benefit of future generations. Since that time, over a hundred masters have appeared who revealed these Treasures and taught them to their disciples, in this way continuing the lineage of Padmasambhava. The master who reveals such treasure is known as the terton , or "treasure revealer." This transmission from Guru Rinpoche through the tertons is called the Terma, the revealed treasure lineage.

These lineages of revealed teachings include the Dzogchen, or Great Completion, teachings taught by Garab Dorje, Shri Simha, Padmasambhava, Jnanasutra, and Vimalamitra.

The lineage transmission that was carried by Padmasambhava originated with the teachings of Samantabhadra, Vajrasattva and the Prince Prahevajra or Garab Dorje, who transmitted the Dzogchen Atiyoga teachings. The latter lived in India a few centuries after the death of the Buddha. Garab Dorje transmitted those teachings to Manjusrimitra and from him to Shrisimha, and then to the Indian-born teachers, Padmasambhava, Jnanasutra, and Vimalamitra. They, together with the Tibetan-born teacher Vairochana, received the transmission of this lineage directly from the aforementioned lineage holders, and in turn transmitted and brought the lineage and teachings to Tibet, thus commencing in Tibet the lineage which continues to the present day.

◎ Mindrol Ling Monastery, one of the main monasteries of the Nyingma Sect.

Initially, the lineage traditions of the Nyingma was based less on institutional structures than on individual lineage transmission, but the Nyingma lineage became more institutionalized later in its history. Nyingma teachers began building great Nyingma monastic centers in the 15th century. The most renowned centers are Mindrol Ling, founded in 1676, Dorje Drak, founded in 1632, Dzogchen, founded in 1685 and Kathok, founded in 1159.

Mindrol Ling monastery is located in Zhanam County in the Shannan Area. It is said that it was built in 1676 on the ruins of an 11th century temple by order of Master Delalhiba who once served as the Fifth Dalai Lama's teacher. It is noted for spreading the teachings and rituals of the Southern Lineage. Monks of all large and small Nyingma monasteries and government officials studied and learned Tibetan culture.

Namah Monastery is located on the southern outskirts of Kangding County of the Sichuan Ganzi Tibet Autonomous Prefecture. The monastery was converted from Nyingma monasteries into Karma Bka-brgyud-pa. It was destroyed after the 17th century. Later it was rebuilt by some lamas and renamed it "Namah Monastery". In 1677 during the reign of Emperor Kang Xi, the original Karma Bka-brgyud-pa was changed into Gelugs

◎ Namah Monastery in the southern outskirts of Kangding County of the Sichuan Ganzi Tibet Autonomous Prefecture

Sect upon the instruction of the Fifth Dalai Lama. The plaque name of the monastery was in the hand of Emperor Qian Long of the Qing Dynasty. Three of the lamas of Namah served as Chiba of the renowned Ganden Monastery. In 1993, the Namah Monastery was designated as a historic relic of priority protection by the Ganzi Tibetan Autonomous Prefecture.

Baiyu (White Jade) Monastery is in the Baiyu County of the Ganzi Tibetan Autonomous Prefecture, Sichuan Province. It was first built in the 17th century by Lhachen Jampa Phuntsog lama. It is one of the six most famous monasteries of the Nyingma Sect. The monastery has a large collection of precious historical relics. The most famous is the sculpture of Master Padmasambhava.

KARDAM SECT (BHA-GDEMSPA)

Kadampa Buddhism is a Mahayana Buddhist school founded by Zongtongpa (1005-1064), a close follower of great Indian Buddhist Master Atisha (AD 982-1054), who came to Tibet to ease the conflicts among Buddhist believers, who preferred the Vinaya school opposed the followers of the Tantric school and vice versa. After the death of Atisha, Zongtongpa built Rwa-sgreng Monastery in 1056, and made it his bodhimandala, thus forming the Kardam sect. His followers are known as 'Kadampas' who followed Atisha's seminal Bodhipathapradipa (Lamp for the Path of Enlightenment) and other works.

The sect divided all human beings into three distinct types. The inferior individual "seeks but the pleasure of Samsara" and is therefore wholly egotistical. The mediocre individual renounces wrongdoing and is indifferent to pleasure, but is concerned with his own peace of mind. The superior individual "seeks a complete end to the entire suffering of others because their suffering belongs to his own samtana, stream of consciousness". The sect strictly observes rules and commandments, putting stress on both open and secret teachings. At the beginning of the 15th century, Tsong-Kha-Pa initiated a reform of the sect and founded the Gelug Sect and Kadampa became part of the Gelug Sect.

SAKYA SECT

The founding of the Sakya sect is attributed to Khon Konchok Gyalpo (1034-1102), who built the great monastery in the Tsang region of central Tibet and founded the Sakya sect in 1073. This area had lots of gray earth, for which reason this seat later known as the Sakya "Gray Earth." As all the walls and most buildings of the Sakya Sect were painted with red, white and black stripes, which respectively symbolize the Wisdom Buddha, the Goddess of Mercy and the Diamond Hand Buddha£¨many scholars called it the Stripe Sect.

The Sakya Sect was passed on through two lines: the family lineage and the Indian lineage. The tradition of the Sakya lineage is closely bound with the Khon family lineage, which originated from celestial beings, according to Sakya history. This unbroken family lineage has continued to the present time from Khon Konchok Gyalpo (1034-1 102), founder of the Sakya tradition.

© The Sakya monastery is in Sakya county, Xigaze Prefecture in South West Tibet.

The Indian lineage of Virupa's teachings continued through Khon Konchok Gyalpo and then to his son Sachen Kunga Nyingpo (1092-1158).

The Sakya Sect of Buddhism teaches people to do good things and avoid doing evils. Unlike other Buddhists, the Sakya Sect followers are allowed to get married, although men are not allowed to approach women after they have children.

The Sakya Sect reached its peak during the Yuan Dynasty (1206-1368), when Chogyel Phagpa was honored as the Imperial Tutor by Emperor Kublai Khan.

As an offering for having been conferred the Hevajra (Kyai-rdo) empowerment, Kublai Khan presented Chogyel Pagpa the rule of the thirteen districts (khri-skor bcu-gsum) of Tibet. Toward the end of the Yuan Dynasty, the position of the Sakya Sect was replaced by Kagyu Sect, which only retained the local political and religious powers.

The Sakya monastery is in Sakya county, Xigaze Prefecture in Southwest Tibet. It is the main seat of the Khon Lineage. Originally, there were a southern Sakya monastery and the northern Sakya monastery. The northern Sakya monastery was founded in the year 1073 by Konchog Gyalpo and the southern Sakya monastery was built by the fifth patriarch Chogyel Pagpa.

◎ Enlightened Hall of Tagong Monastery in Kangding County of Sichuan Ganzi
Tibetan Autonomous Prefecture.

It became a political, cultural and religious center of Tibet in the
12th century. The monastery boasts a rich collection of Buddhist
scriptures and rare relics as well as books on astrology, calendar,
medicine, history, biography, philosophy, music, grammar and
rhetoric. For its inestimably valuable historical relics, it is widely
acclaimed by Chinese and foreign scholars as the "second
Dunhuang".

Tagong Monastery is in Kangding County of Sichuan Ganzi
Tibetan Autonomous Prefecture. It was built in the 18th century
by Padeng Dojie Lama of the Sakya Sect. It is the earliest Sakya
monastery built in a pastoral area. The monastery houses a lot of

historical relics. The most important of all is the Enlightened Hall, in which there is a statue of Sakyamuni brought to Tibet by Princess Wencheng. The monastery was listed as a historical site for priority protection by the autonomous prefecture's government.

KAGYU SECT

Founded in the 11th century, the Kagyu Sect stresses the study of Tantrism and advocates that Tantrist tenets be passed down orally from one generation to another. Hence the name Gagyu, which in the Tibetan language means "passing down orally." Marba and Milha Riba are the founders of the Gagyu Sect. As they wore white monk robes when practicing Buddhism, scholars also call it White Sect. The sect holds that all things in the world are empty, even the heart. It is noted for its hard practice, but it does not stress much written sutras.

The three main Tantric Yidam practices that are unique to the Kagyu Sect are Vajrayogini (rdo rje phag mo), Cakrasambhava (khor lo sde mchog), and Gyalwa Gyamtso (rgyal ba rgya mtsho).

In the early years, the White Sect was divided into many sub-sects. The most powerful were Phaktru Kagyu and Karma

Kagyu, whose senior monks were granted honorary titles by the Yuan and Ming dynasties and ordained to control the local political power in Tibet.

The main seats of the Kagyu Sect are Zhigung Till Monastery in Congkar County of Mochu and the Babang Monastery in Dege of Sichuan.

The Babang Monastery, Beh-bung genpa or Palpung Gompa is in Dege County of the Ganzi Tibetan Autonomous Prefecture in Sichuan Province. It is the largest Kagyu monastery in Ganzi. It was founded by the eighth Tai Situpa in 1727. All the living buddhas of the Babang monastery were very

◎ The Babang Monastery, Beh-bung genpa or Palpung Gompa is in Dege County of the Ganzi Tibetan Autonomous Prefecture in Sichuan Province.

knowledgeable, with great attainments in Buddhist theories. They have left many valuable works, which are the most valuable treasure of the sect. Situpa has the longest lineage, with 12 incarnations up to the present. The Babang monastery has a large collection of historical relics, with many rare ones. The monastery was listed as a historical relic for priority protection by Sichuan Province in 1981.

GELUG SECT

The Gelug Sect was started by Zongkhapa (1357-1419) following a period of religious reform to redress the declining situation of all sects of Buddhism that featured lax rules and discipline, distraction of monks by secular life and violations of monastic commandments.

As the Gelug monks usually wear yellow peach-shaped hats, it is also known as the Yellow Sect.

This Buddhist sect, as suggested by the name, which means Order of Excellence or Virtuous Order in the Tibetan language, requires its followers to strictly abide by its discipline, not to marry and keep away from economic activities and strictly observe the organizational and management rules of monasteries so that they would not be manipulated by secular nobles.

Zongkhapa gave equal importance to exoteric and esoteric forms of Buddhism, with exoteric preceding esoteric form. The sect was founded on the doctrines of "everything is caused by nature void", preaching that all things in the world are all in causal relationships and changing under given conditions. Apart from these, there is nothing else and there is no objective independent entity, hence "immateriality of own nature".

After the death of Zongkhapa, his disciples built a number of monasteries such as the Zhaibung Monastery, the Sera Monastery and the Zhaxilhunbu Monastery, as the influence of the Gelug Sect spread.

In 1542 during the 21st year of the reign of Emperor Jia Jing of the Ming dynasty, the Gelug Sect introduced in the living buddha reincarnation system, with Sonam Gyatso put in control of the Zhaibung Monastery. In 1578 during the 6th year of the reign of Emperor Wan Li of the Ming Dynasty, Sonam Gyatso met with the Mongol King Altan Khan in Qinghai, who conferred the title ""Dalai Lama", meaning Ocean Of Wisdom, to become the third Dalai Lama. Sonam Gyatso (1543-1588) was again conferred the title in the 15th year of Emperor Wan li. The practice of conferring the title "Dalai Lama" became established when Emperor Shun Zhi of the Qing Dynasty bestowed the same title on the Great Fifth (the fifth Dalai Lama, Ngawang Losang Gyatso) in 1652. In 1713, in the 52nd year of his rule, Emperor Kang Xi of the Qing Dynasty conferred the title of Panchen Erdeni to the fifth Panchen Lama. The Gelug Sect gradually became the leading religious sect in Tibet. It is held in great esteem by the people of the Tibet Autonomous Region, and has remained influential for six centuries.

The main seats of the Gelug Sect are the Gandain Monastery, the Zhaibung Monastery, the Sera Monastery and Zhaxilhunbu Monastery in Tibet and the Tar Monastery in Qinghai, and the Labrang Monastery in Gansu. The Fifth Dalai Lama also expanded the Potala Palace in Lhasa as residence of Dalai Lamas. There are also some smaller sects of Tibetan Buddhism.

ZHAXILHUNBU MONASTERY

The Zhaxilhunbu Monastery, located on the southern slope of the Nyimari Mountain northwest of the city of Xigaze, is one of the six major monasteries of the Gelug Sect, and the largest one in western Tibet.

Gendain Zhuba, the most famous disciple of Master Zongkhapa and the 1st Dalai Lama, built the Zhaxilhunbu Monastery. In 1600, the 4th Dalai Lama Lobsang Qoigyi

Gyaincain expanded the monastery. Following nearly constant reconstruction thereafter, the Zhaxilhunbu Monastery stands at an impressive scale today. Covering a construction area of 300,000 square meters, the monastery housed some 4,000 monks during its peak period.

The Zhaxilhunbu Monastery boasts four Lhadrang palace residences for Panchen Erdeni. In 1660 when the 4th Panchen Lobsang Qoigyi Gyaincain succeeded as the 16th abbot of the monastery, he had the monastery expanded. In 1645, Gushri Khan granted Lobsang Qoigyi Gyaincain the title of Panchen Pokto (Pokto means a "wise and brave man" in Mongolian). In 1713, the Qing court granted the title of Panchen Erdeni to the 5th Panchen Lobsang Yexei. From then on, the Panchen earned his official position and the Zhaxilhunbu Monastery became his residence.

Qambaling Monastery is in the Qamdo prefecture of Tibet. When Xangsheng Xirab Sangbo, son of the chief of a 1,000-Household Office in Riwoqe, finished his studies in the Sera Monastery, he had the Qambaling Monastery built in Chamdo according to the will of Gyiachaogyi, the first disciple of Zongkhapa, in 1437. It is the largest Gelug sect monastery in the area.

◎ Qambaling Monastery.

When the 3rd Parbalha became the 14th abbot of the Qambaling Monastery, he set a precedent whereby succeeding generations of the Living Buddha Parbalha became the chief abbot of the monastery, and leader of its five major Living Buddhas. The 6th, 7th, 8th and 9th Living Buddha Parbalha all received honorific titles from the Qing Dynasty emperors. Qambaling Monastery grew into the largest monastery of the Gelug Sect. Parbalha Geleinamgyi, vice-chairman of the National People's Congress of the People's Republic of China, is the 11th living Buddha Parbalha.

GANDAIN MONASTERY

The Gandain Monastery on the southern bank of the Lhasa River in Dagze county, Lhasa, was the earliest and the biggest seat of Gelug Sect. It was built after Zongkhapa, founder of the Gelug Sect, pioneered the Grand Summons Ceremony in Lhasa in 1409. The event marked the official formation of the Gelug Sect of Tibetan Buddhism. Of the six monasteries belonging to the Gelug Sect, the Gandain is the most important and the largest. During the Qing Dynasty (1644-1911), the imperial court named it Yongshou Monastery while the Tibetans called it Dgav-ldan mam-par rgyal-bavi-gling.

© Gandain Monastery.

The Gandain Monastery has a rich collection of historical relics, including one hamlet inlaid with gold and silver gems and written with words in the Han Chinese, Manchurian, Mongolian and Tibetan languages. It was a gift from Qing Dynasty Emperor Qian Long in 1757. Other relics include the set of Gangyur of Tibetan Tripitaka, which is written in gold powder ink, and 24 pieces of silk tangka paintings of the 16 arhats and the four Heavenly Deva Kings. In recognition of its important role in religion, art, politics and cultural relics, the Gandain Monastery was made one of the cultural relics units brought under state protection in 1961.

ZHAIBUNG MONASTERY

The Zhaibung Monastery, which in Tibetan is called Duimi or Gyimi monastery and means "an auspicious land", sits at the southern slope gully of the Gebeiwoze Mountain about 10 km west of downtown Lhasa. It was built by Jamyang Qoigyi Zhaxi Bendain, a favorite disciple of Zongkhapa, founder of the Gelug (Yellow) Sect of Tibetan Buddhism. It is one of the six Gelug monasteries in China.

The Zhaibung Monastery is composed of the Coqen Hall, the four Zhacang colleges (called Losailing, Deyang, Ngaba and

◎ Zhaibung Monastery.

Gomang Zhacangs) and the Gandain Phodrang (Palace).

The Zhaibung Monastery holds many kinds of religious activities to honor large Buddhist memorial days and the Repentance Day, which falls on the 15th and 30th days of each Tibetan month. There are also activities for monks and lay people to celebrate together. The largest of these include the Shoton

(Sour Milk Drinking) Festival on the 30th day of the 6th Tibetan month.

The Zhaibung Monastery preserves close to 10,000 ancient classics, more than 100 volumes of Gangyur and 100 volumes of Dangyur, and hundreds of volumes of hand-copied works by Zongkhapa and two of his disciples.

SERA MONASTERY

The Sera Monastery is located at the southern slope of the Serawoze Mountain in the northern suburbs of Lhasa, the monastery covers an area that was once strewn with wild roses

© Sera Monastery.

called Sewa. It was built by Sagya Yeshes (1354-1435, who was given the title of the Great Mercy Prince of Dharma during the Ming Dynasty), one of the eight disciples of Zongkhapa, founder of the Gelug Sect of Tibetan Buddhism, in 1419. In 1962, it was made a cultural relics unit subject to protection at the Tibet Autonomous Region level. In 1982, the monastery was put under national protection.

The Sera Monastery is grand in scale, covering an area of 114,964 square meters. Its building complex is composed of Buddha halls, sutra halls, Zhacang (Buddhist colleges), residences for monks, Kamcun, and Lhadrang palace residences for major Living Buddhas Cermoiling and Razheng. Most important are the Coqen Hall, the Meba Zhacang, the Ngaba Zhacang, and the Gyi Zhacang. In the early period of its existence, the monastery was composed mainly of the Meba Zhacang and Ngaba Zhacang.

The Sera Monastery has a rich collection of cultural relics, many of which are considered to be of state class. They include statues of the Buddha, tangka paintings, frescoes, Buddhist scriptures, Buddhist objects and sacrificial articles.

RAMOCHE MONASTERY

Ramoche Monastery, located in the northeastern section of

Lhasa, was commissioned, constructed and consecrated at the same time as Jokhang Monastery. Built under the aegis of the Tang Dynasty Princess Wencheng, the gate of the monastery faces east to show the princess' nostalgia for her homeland. The temple was known as Gyuiada Ramo Chezolhakang, meaning a "monastery incarnated from a Han tiger." In Tibetan, Jokhang means a major Buddha while Rachome means a minor Buddha.

Enshrined in the major hall of Ramoche Monastery is a statue of Sakyamuni, which Princess Wencheng took with her to Tibet from Chang'an (today's Xi'an), while the major hall of the Jokhang Monastery houses the statue of Sakyamuni taken from Kathmandu to Tibet by the Nepalese Princess Bhributi.

One of the temple's prized artifacts is the life-sized statue of Sakyamuni in his 12th year. The Wencheng Princess brought it from the capital Chang'an during the Tang Dynasty. As one of the precious cultural relics of Tibet, the statue is now placed in Jokhang Monastery (Da Zhao Si), 500 meters (0.31 miles) south of Ramoche Monastery. Residing within the Ramoche Monastery is the life-sized statue of Sakyamuni in his eighth year. Carried into Tibet by the Nepalese Chizun Princess, this figure is regarded as the greatest saint in Ramoche Monastery.

Nowadays, the temple has become the very place for the

Tibetan monks to study Mi Zong (one of the sects of Buddhism).

The Lhasa Upper Tantric College for monks of the Gelug Sect has been established in Ramoche Monastery, and the college abbot also serves as the abbot of the monastery.

TAR MONASTERY

The Tar Monastery, which means "Holy Place for the 100,000-Body Maitreya Buddha," is located in the Lotus Flower

© Tar aMonastay.

Mountain south of Lusha'er town. Huangzhong County, Qinghai Province.

Zongkhapa, founder of the Gelug (Yellow) Sect of Tibetan

Buddhism, was born in the place where the Tar Monastery is located. The 3rd Dalai Lama Soinam Gyamco initiated construction of the monastery in Zongkhapa's honor.

Architecture. Of the six major Gelug sect monasteries, the Tar Monastery boasts more halls built in the Tibetan, Han and Hui styles. The Grand Gold Tile Hall is of Han palace style, with three-tiered roofs adorned with patterns of clouds and lotus petals, pagodas, gold animals and bronze bells. Inside the hall stands an 11-meter silver pagoda enshrined with the gilded statue of Zongkhapa, founder of the Gelug Sect. On the lotus altar are perennially burning butter lamps. The inscribed handwriting of the Qing Emperor Qian Long adorns a horizontal bar.

The Grand Sutra Hall, covering an area of 1,981 square meters, is propped up by 168 pillars, 60 of which are built inside the walls. Each pillar is carved with beautiful patterns and wrapped in colorful rugs. Numerous cushions are in the hall where thousands of lamas sit while reciting Buddhist scriptures. Nearly 1,000 gilded bronze statues of Buddha enshrine the four walls.

The Tar Monastery is also famous for its butter sculptures, frescoes and duisui embroidery. Butter sculptures are most often of Buddha, other figures and flowers.

LABRANG MONASTERY

The Labrang Monastery sits on the northern bank of Daxia River in west Xiabe County, Gannan Tibetan Nationality Autonomous Prefecture in Gansu Province. It was built by the First Living Buddha Jamyang in 1709 at the request of Beleg Chakhan Dainzin of the Qianshou Banner of the Mongol Hoshod in Qinghai. It includes six major Zhacangs (colleges), 48 Buddha halls and residences for Living Buddhas, and some 500 residential quarters for monks.

The six Buddhist colleges (Zhacang) in the monastery are: Tiesam Lamwa, Jumaiba, Judoba, Dingker, Manba and Jido Zhacangs.

The Tiesam Lamwa Zhacang, also known as the Grand Sutra Hall, is where monks with the monastery study the open sect theories of Tibetan Buddhism.

The Jumaiba Zhacang, the Lower Tantric College, is where monk students study Tantric teachings and receive abhiseka.

The Judoba Zhacang is the Upper Tantric College where students further their study of the teachings of the secrete sect of Tibetan Buddhism.

The Dingker Zhacang was built by the 2nd Living Buddha Jamyang some 200 years ago in accordance with the instructions

© Labrang Moanastery.

of the 6th Panchen Lobsang Huadain Yexei.

The Manba Zhacang is the medical college created by the 2nd Living Buddha Jamyang. It follows the style of the Yaowangshan Monastic Medical School in Lhasa and specializes in cultivating monks steeped in Tibetan medicine.

PUNING MONASTERY

The Puning Monastery is in the northeastern part of the Chengde Summer Resort in Hebei Province. Built in 1855, the 20th year of the reign of Emperor Qian Long, it covers 33,000 square meters. As it was built in memory of the victory in suppressing the dawalqi rebellion of Jungar, it was named Puning, meaning there would be peace everywhere under heaven.

It is a Gelug monastery modeled on the Bsamyas Monastery featuring Han and Tibetan in architectural style. The central building-the Mahayana Hall houses a statue of Sahasrabhuja-sahasranetra-avalokitesvara (thousand arm and thousand eye Avalokitesvara). Carved in wood and painted with golden coat, it stands 22.28 meters, weighing about 110 tons. Well proportionately shaped, it looks very beautiful, presenting a strong soul-stirring impression.

HONGPO MONASTERY

Also known as "Gaindan Yangbajain Forest Temple", is in Deqin County, Yunnan Province. It was first built in 1515, the 9th year of the reign of Emperor Zhengde of the Ming Dynasty. The monastery was pulled down for its opposition to Tibetan religious King Gusikhan. It was restored in 1753, the 18th year of the reign of Emperor Qian Long. Once it served as a monastery of the Gegyu (white sect) Sect and was later converted into a monastery of the Nyingma (red) Sect. Later it was again converted into a monastery of the Yellow Sect. It is one of three major monasteries of Tibetan Buddhism in Deqin County. It preserves a precious plaque "Hua Xing Nan Bang", meaning pacifying the southern neighbor, granted by the imperial court during the reign of Emperor Xian Feng of the Qing Dynasty.

JOKHANG MONASTERY

The Jokhang Monastery is in the middle of the Bajiao Street of Lhasa. Built in 647, it occupies an area of 13,000 square meters, with a building floor space of 25,100 square meters. It is one of the earliest Buddhist structures in Lhasa. Zongkhapa, founder of the Gelug Sect, pioneered the Grand Summons Ceremony at the Jokhang Monastery in Lhasa in 1409.

© Jokhang Monastery.

The monastery preserves the Sakyamuni statue presented to Princess Wen Cheng by the Tang Emperor, the willow tree planted by Princess Wen Cheng and other precious objects symbolizing the good relations between the Han and Tibetan people.

The grand lot-drawing ceremony was held in the monastery to identify the incarnation of the 10th Penchen Lama.

SAMYE MONASTERY

Samye is on the northern bank of the Yalung Zambu River in Zanam County, Shannan Prefecture in Tibet. It is widely believed that the corner stone was laid in 767 and it was completed

© Samye Monastery.

in 799. The monastery was designed on the plan of the Odantapuri temple in India (present-day Bihar), and mirrors the structure of the universe according to Buddhist cosmology. The central temple represents Mt. Sumeru, the mythical mountain at the centre of the cosmos. Around it are four temples called 'ling', which represent the four continents and to the right and left of each of these are smaller temples, representing eight sub-continents.

It was destroyed by fire several times and after each fire it was rebuilt.

XIALU MONASTERY

The Xialu Monastery is situated in Xigaze. Built by Chetsun Sherab Jungnay in 1087, the architecture is of typical combination of the Tibetan and Chinese styles.

In 1320, Buton Rinpoche (1290-1364), one of Tibet's greatest scholars was invited to the monastery as abbot and founded his sect known as Butonpa or Shalupa.

© Tangka.

Baiju Monastery (Polchoi or Palkor Monasstery)

Located in the Town of Gyangze, Gyangze County of Xigaze Prefecture, it was built by Yaodan Gongsangpa and Zongkhapa's disciple Khedrub Je in 1439. It is dwelt by three religious sects:

© Baiju Monastery.

Sakya, Gedan and Gelug. The frescoes, statues and sculptures in the monastery are exquisite, succinct and life-like. The monastery is well regarded as an art museum.

ZUONI MONASTERY

Situated on a platform north of the Zuoni County, Gansu Province, it was built in about 1269. In 1713,Emperor Kang Xi of the Qing dynasty granted a name plaque "Meditation Monastery". So it is also known as "Meditation Monastery".

The monastery keeps a lot of Buddhist images and Pattra leaf sutras as well as scripts by Zongkhapa.

YONGHEGONG LAMASERY

Yonghegong Lamasery, a renowned lama temple of the Yellow Sect of Lamaism, is situated in the northeastern part of Beijing. It was originally built in 1694 during the 33rd year of Emperor Kang Xi of the Qing Dynasty.

The main gate faces south, and on its 480-meter-long north-south axis are five main halls and annexes laid out tastefully over an area of 66,400 square meters. They include a glaze-tiled arch, Gate of Peace Declaration (Zhaotaimen), Devaraja Hall (Tianwangdian), which was formerly the entrance to Yongzheng's imperial palace, Hall of Harmony and Peace (Yonghegong), Hall of Everlasting Protection (Yongyoudian), Hall of the Wheel of the Law (Falundian) and Pavilion of Eternal Happiness (Wanfuge).

◎ Statue of Maitreya (the Smiling Buddha) in Yonghegong Lamasery.

The Pavilion of Eternal Happiness is the largest structure in Yonghegong Lamasery. It is also known as a big Buddha Pavilion. Standing more than 30 meters, it is of entire wooden structure in the style of Liao and Jin dynasties. Standing in the center of the pavilion is a 26-meter-tall statue of Maitreya (the Smiling Buddha), which is carved out of a single sandalwood tree 8 meters in diameter, with 8 meters underground and 18 meters above ground. The whole statue weighs about 100 tons. It is said that the big tree was shipped through thousands of miles to China from Southeast Asia.

Yonghegong is not only a famous Buddhist shrine but also a treasure-house of Han, Manchu, Mongolian and Tibetan arts.

KARTO (KATHOK) MONASTERY

The Karto Monastery, located 20 kilometers north of the Baiyu County of the Ganzi Tibetan Prefecture of Sichuan Province is the earliest and biggest monastery in Ganzi area and the No. 1 of the six major seats of Nyingma Sect of Tibetan Buddhism. It was built in 1160 by eminent Monk Gardampa Desheshiba. It is also one of the five temples of Dege Tusi.

The Monastery houses many precious historical relics, including the gold hat, four-window sedan, a complete set of

◎ A Bird's-eye View of Yonghegong.

ritual instruments granted by Emperor Kang Xi when a senior monk of the monastery was summoned to Beijing in the 18th century. In 1750, during the 25th year of the reign of Emperor Qian Long, the monastery built a sutra printing hall and a cultivation hall. The Monastery has trained a large number of high-ranking monks.

GENGQING MONASTERY(GOMCHHEN GONPA)

Gengqing Monastery is in Dege County of the Sichuan Ganzi Tibetan Autonomous Prefecture. It was built on the basis of a sutra hall put up in 1445 during the 13th year of the reign of Emperor Zhen Tong of the Ming Dynasty by the highly accomplished Tangtong Gyalpo together with the first generation of the Dege clan. In 1729, a sutra Printing Academy, simply as Dege Scripture Printing House, was added by Queji Dengbazeren, the 12th headman and the 6th dharma-raja of Dege. The monastery does not follow the practice of reincarnation of living Buddha and the Tusi of Dege clan always serves as the abbot.

A treasury house of Tibetan culture and arts, the scripture printing house keeps more than 290000 engraved blocks of religious books including classics from different sects of Tibetan Buddhism, history, literature and art, medical, technology and science, language, astronomical and calendar-arithmatical book editions in Tibetan, all together containing over 500 million characters and the Dege block edition of The Great Scriptures cut in the Qing Dynasty is especially well-known.

The monastery was listed as a historical relic for priority protection by the State Council in 1996.

CHAPTER FOUR
PALI LANGUAGE BUDDHISM OF CHINA

1. Introduction of Pali language Buddhism into Yunnan

Pali language Buddhism is also known as Southern Buddhism or Theravada, as it was originated in Sri Lanka, Myanmar, Thailand, Cambodia and Laos. According to historical records, King Asoka at Pataliputta (now Patna, India) of India convened the third council of Buddhism in about 250 BC and sent missionaries to neighboring countries to spread Theravada. Asoka's son, the monk Mahinda, and others went to Sri Lanka and founded the Theravada Buddhist Group centered at the great monastery of Mahavihara. In about the 1st millennium AD, the

Theravada Fourth Council was held in Sri Lanka, which recorded in the Pali language the Tipitaka of Theravada.

In 410-432, Pali Buddhism scholar of ancient India Ven. Buddhaghosa came to Sri Lanka, where he collated the various Sinhalese commentaries on the Canon - drawing primarily on the Maha Atthakatha (Great Commentary) preserved at the Mahavihara, and translated his work into Pali. As a cornerstone to his work, Buddhaghosa composed the Visuddhimagga (The Path of Purity). Up to the 14th century, Theravada became national creed in Sri Lanka, Myanmar, Thailand, Cambodia and Laos.

Southern Buddhism is close to primitive Buddhism in doctrines, stressing the interpretation of the Buddhist teachings. The core of the doctrines is "Trilaksana (three aspects of the nature of a thing), that is, impermanence (anitya), suffering (duhkha) and no self (anatman). Southern Buddhists worship teeth, pagoda and the bodhi-tree. They stressed the study of the rules or discipline, meditation and philosophy and the eight holy or correct ways, or gates out of suffering into nirvana, which are: (1) Samyag-drsti, correct views in regard to the Four Axioms, and freedom from the common delusion. (2) Samyak-samkalpa, correct thought and purpose. (3) Samyag-vac, correct speech, avoidance of false and idle talk. (4) Samyak-karmanta, correct deed, or conduct, getting rid of all improper action so as to dwell in purity. (5) Smnyag-ajiva, correct livelihood or occupation, avoiding the five immoral occupations. (6) Samyag-vyayama, correct zeal, or energy in uninterrupted progress in the way of nirvana. (7) Samyak-smrti, correct remembrance, or memory, which retains the true and excludes the false. (8) Samyak-samadhi, correct meditation, absorption, or abstraction. They pay special attention to meditation and retain some of the rules and discipline of the primitive Buddhism, such as contributing to the needs of communities, no food after noon and retreat during the rainy seasons.

Southern Buddhism uses scriptures in the Pali language and commemorates the birth, enlightenment and nirvana of the Buddha, calling it Vaisakha.

Southern Buddhism is popular only in the Xishuangbanna area in Southern or southwestern Yunnan and among the communities of Dai, Achang, De'ang and part of the Wa people in Dehong, Lincang, Simao and Baoshan areas. The religion has had a big impact on the social, cultural, arts and education of these ethnic minorities, so much so that it has formed a Buddhist cultural sphere represented by the Dais that is of particular features in morality, mental state, customs and conventions, language and education, calendar, health and medicine, painting, building structures, music and dance.

All the people (nearly 900,000) of the Dai nationality in southern or southwestern Yunnan are Pali Buddhism believers. It is the earliest Chinese minority to accept and understand Buddhism. It has the biggest influence on neighboring people. Xishuangbanna area is the earliest to introduce Buddhism and has therefore become the center of Buddhism in southern or southwestern Yunnan.

Southern Buddhism spread into Xishuangbanna area in Yunnan in about the 7th century from Mengrun of Thailand via Jingdong of Burma, far later than Mahayana Buddhism.

The Buddhist circles of Xishuangbanna area have fixed the date for the beginning of the introduction of Southern Buddhism at 86 (724) of the Dai calendar. But at the beginning, people did not really understand Buddhism. This, plus frequent wars, did not make the religion spread. In 1180, Southern Buddhism found its way into Xishuangbanna again and that should really be the date for the introduction of Southern Buddhism. But the religion did not become widespread until 1277.

Southern Buddhism did not assume a certain scale and

flourish until the Ming Dynasty. When a Myanmar princess was married to the 25th Yunnan magistrate in 1569, the King of Myanmar sent a Buddhist mission to Yunnan, sending with them Buddhist scriptures and statues. The second year, the Myanmar Princess built a big temple known as Golden Lotus Temple and only by then Southern Buddhism entered into a period of restoration.

Southern Buddhism spread into the Dehong area in about 13th century. Dai King Zhao Wu Ding built a Buddhist tower in the locality. The tower was built and rebuilt for seven times before being expanded into a big golden tower, known as Jiele Golden Pagoda, a 47-meter-high main tower among a cluster of 16 smaller ones. It is believed to contain an interred bone of the Buddha.

2. Sects of Yunnan Pali Buddhism

RUN SECT

The Run Sect of Southern Buddhism derived its name from "Meng Run" in ancient times, which is the present-day Chiang-Mai via which this sect of Southern Buddhism was introduced into Xishuangbanna from Sri Lanka. Main followers of this sect are in Xishuangbanna and Lincang area.

DUOLIE SECT

This sect of Southern Buddhism belongs to Arannanikaya. Believers are not very strict with self-cultivation and religious rituals. They call temple "Zhuang", which is built several hundred meters from villages. Women can also be ordained to become sramanerika (female novice), who live in special rooms reserved in the Zhuang. Monks observe the rule of no food after noon. But they do not care about eating chickens, fish and other meats that are not killed by themselves. In the past, the rules had it that monks could not ride horses or a sedan when going out or hanging out at rural fairs. They could only go out with an umbrella. But now, they can go out by air or by boat. When sleeping, monks only cover themselves with a blanket, without any matting. They wear kasaya only during religious ceremonies.

BAIZHUANG SECT

Also called "Geng Long", this sect was introduced into Mangshi, Ruili, Zhefang, Yingjiang, Longchuan and Lianshan areas of Dehong Prefecture, Yunnan Province, from Burma in the middle period of the Ming Dynasty. Monks of this sect are allowed to breed and slaughter domestic animals and poultry and also to smoke and drink alcohol. Temples are built inside villages and have their own property. This sect has more followers among the Dai, Achang, De'ang (Benglong) ethnic minorities in Dehong.

ZUODI SECT

This sect was founded by Wa La, a Mandala bhiksu of Burma. It was introduced into Yunnan through two lines toward the end of the Qing Dynasty. One was Rangoon-Mangshi of Dehong; the other was Nan Han of Burma to Ruili of Dehong and Lincang and Mengding areas.

The sect is very strict with monastic rules and disciplines.

Monks are not allowed to eat meat or have food after noon or breed domestic animals and poultry. Slaughters are not allowed to enter temples. When sleeping, monks do not use mats or mosquito nets. Temples are built outside villages. Women can become sramanerika (female novice) and they must strictly observe rules and discipline. Female novices live in rooms specially reserved for them. But the sect is too strict with rules and discipline to attract so many followers. It was later edged out by the Baizhuang Sect. In 1915, the sect returned to Burma and the followers in Yunnan were converted to Duolie sect.

3. Life and Customs of Yunnan Pali Buddhism

Dai boys are usually sent by their parents to Buddhist temples to become "keyongs" (novices) at age 7 or 8. They do not shave their heads or wear kasaya or live in temples. They only learn how to read and write in the Dai language. Now the ancient Pali language has been replaced by the modern Dai language. They also learn some simple Buddhist rules and rituals. At about ten years old, they may apply to become monks.

To become a monk is a big matter for Dai boys, because only those who have become monks can be regarded as real men and qualified to join the community and respected accordingly. Those who have not become monks are regarded as "barbarians" and therefore rejected by the community and no women would marry them. When a keyong is upgraded into a monk, the parents would invite the preceptor (Wopo) to a celebration feast. The keyong would have his head and brows shaved and ride a horse or sit on the back of somebody to the temple. The ordination ceremony is presided over by a Bhiksu. The keyong would bow to the Buddhist image, scriptures and monks before being ordained and then get a monk's robe, thus acquiring the status as a "Pa". There are no certificates for monks of the Theravada in Yunnan. Neither do monks have scars burned on their heads. Apart from learning how to read and write and recite Buddhist scriptures, the Pa's have to do all the chores in the temple, such as fetching water, cutting firewood, cleaning the temple, doing cooking, feeding domestic animals and attending to senior monks and going out of the temple to beg for alms. Pa's are not allowed to sit or eat together with Bhiksus. They can eat only after Bhiksus finish. There is also a low rank below Pa, for boys who have just been sent to the temples. They are called panon (child monk) in some temples. After they study the Buddhist scriptures and rituals for one or two years and have some ground in Buddhist paintings, they would become Pa's. The duration to be a panon or pa can be long or short, with the shortest being one or two years and the longest being seven or eight years, all depending on themselves. It is also very simple to return to secular life. It only requires the application by their parents and the consent of the Bhiksus. Modern temples are more relaxed in the management of Pa's, even allowing them to go to schools in ordinary times and return to the temple on winter and summer vocations.

When a pa reaches 20, he may be ordained as a Bhiksu. There are 227 commandments for Bhiksus. The ordination ceremony is performed at an ordination altar. The candidate to be ordained wears decorations and goes to the homes of his parents to enjoy for the last time before returning to the ordination altar, takes off the secular clothes and decorations and put on yellow robe and then becomes a Bhiksu. This is the practice of how Sakyamuni became a monk. The formal Buddhist robe is made by linking yellow cloth strips,

◎ Take off secular clothes and put on monk's robe to become a "keyong" (novice).

◎ Ceremony of ordination for children of Tai families.

◎ Music band for Buddhist activities in a Dai village.

seven horizontal and nine vertical. On the day of being upgraded to a Bhiksu, he wears the yellow robe and holds a bowl. Relatives and well-wishers would put gold, silver and pearls into the bowl as a form of greeting. The new Bhiksu then walks among a passage covered with white cloth, symbolizing the beginning of waling toward a superhuman realm. Bhiksus are free from doing manual labor, but they are responsible for directing novices in reciting Buddhist scriptures and learn religious rules and rites. Bhiksus themselves must firmly abide by the Buddhist rules and work hard in self-cultivation.

WATER SPLASHING FESTIVAL

The Water Splashing Festival is originated in Brahman of ancient India. The Brahmans used to go to the holy rivers at the beginning of a year to take a bath to wash away sins and evils and pray for good luck. The Brahman followers also hold that that is a day for the Sakra-devanam Indra to come down from heaven to see whether secular people are kind or evil.

The festival is held by the Dai Nationality in the sixth month of the Dai calendar (in the middle of April). The Water Splashing Festival generally lasts three to four days. The first day is a day of greeting; the second day is a day of descend; the third day is a day of inspection; the fourth day is a day of ascend, returning to the heaven. Legend has it that when Sakra-devanam Indra drops from heaven, it usually rides an animal and has something in hand and the animals and things in hand are different from year to year. The animals include birds, horse, cattle or dragon and things in hand include weapons, torch or kettle. People can tell the harvest of the year according to what Sakra-devanam Indra rides and what things in his hand. If he rides a cow, with a kettle in hand, it means that the year would have abundant rain and there would be a good harvest; if he holds a torch in hand, it means there would be a drought. After announcing the results of the prediction, the Brahman followers would splash water to one another, as a way of praying for rain and good harvest.

When Buddhism spread into Southeast Asia and the Dai

area in China's Yunnan Province, the water splashing festival changed its original religious meaning, which was replaced by Buddhist stories. Water splashing is no longer mainly a way of praying for rains and good harvest. It became a Buddha bathing festival. The Buddhist legend has gradually been mingled with the customs of the Dai people since their conversion to Buddhism. The modern festival combines the Flower Collecting Festival and the Water Festival. Many other Dai myths have been added to it; one of them is the dance of the seven beautiful Dai women exorcising the fire fiend. Women begin the festival by cleaning their bamboo abodes and village streets and by washing their furniture and clothing. The young people pick wild flowers from

◎ Religious activity of Southern Buddhism believers.

◎ Students of the Xishuangbanna College of the Yunnan Provincial Buddhism Institute at a water-splashing ceremony.

the fields and lay them before Buddhist statues enshrined in nearby temples, pile up sand in the shape of pagodas in the fields, and sit around an eminent monk to listen to his recitation of Buddhist sutras. At noontime, a statue of the Buddha is moved into the courtyard and water is brought from the river to wash it. Afterwards, the villagers, old and young, men and women, splash water on each other as an expression of goodwill. Many people are drenched during the process, but nonetheless feel happy, for they believe this ritual can bring them good luck. Boys and girls throw finely embroidered purses to each other and person he or she is in love with.

At the same time villagers also participate in dragon boat racing, go to country fairs, dance elephant foot drum and peacock dances, parade floats and let off fireworks and hang out lanterns. The activities last deep into the night. Similar activities are also popular among people of Bulang, A'chang, De'ang and Wa minorities in Dehong, Lincang and Honghe.

OFFERING WHITE ELEPHANT FESTIVAL

This is a pure Buddhist festival. Originated from the stories of the Buddha, the festival celebrates the spirit of devotion and generosity.

The festival is held in January or February every year. According to records of Buddhist scriptures in the Dai language, there was a white elephant in a rich state of ancient India. It is very magic, said to bring luck, happiness to man. As the state had such an elephant, the state enjoyed great prosperity, with the people secured of peace and stability. Later, a neighboring state was in the grip of drought. Starvation was everywhere. At this moment, the state asked the rich state for presenting its white elephant so that rain would fall. The prince of the state promised and gave the white elephant to that state suffering from hunger. But the move met great opposition from ministers, who told this to the King. The prince was then driven out of the palace and went in hiding with his wife and children. While engaging in

◎ Dance of Southern Buddhism.

self cultivation, he was tortured by Brahmans. But, instead of taking revenge, he returned evil with kindness. He even gave up his wife and children to Brahman. His generosity moved the heavenly god, who helped him reunited with his wife and children. Brahman received due punishment. The prince was the former self of Sakyamuni.

The White Elephant Offering Festival in the Dai area lasts three days. People make white elephants with bamboo chips, plastered with white cotton and decorated with a golden saddle and other decorative objects. In the first two days, the people would gather at a Buddhist temple to hear the recitation of

Buddhist scriptures. On the third day, the people in their best would take to streets in a parade, holding up the bamboo elephants as well as paper deer and cattle and Buddhist images. A large crowd would follow the parade, shouting "Sa, Sa and Sa" while walking. Then they would throw up popped rice into the air. Some people participating in the parade wear masks and some hold color flags and fresh flowers and some beat elephant foot drums and dance. When the parade reaches the temple, people would place the things they carry as a present to the Buddha. Returning home, the people would slaughter pigs or cattle and treated themselves to a feast.

The White Elephant Offering Festival is the most popular in the Gengma and Jinggu areas.

FIREWOOD BURNING FESTIVAL

It falls on the 15th day of the first month of the Lunar Calendar. On the day, Buddhist believers collect firewood and pile them up in the temple. On the evening, the monks of all temples gather in the temple, reciting scriptures and then a senior monk light the firewood, amidst the let-off of firecrackers. Crowds of people around cheer. The scripture reciting monks led by the senior Monk would go to a forest near the village and stay there for seven days. They recite scriptures in the day and sleep under the trees at night. At the end of the seventh day, they gather at a square to recite scriptures. When the Sun rises, the festival ends. The monks return to their respective temples.

The legend has it that a long, long time ago, there was a kind couple. The man was called Zhan Luo and the wife was called Popa. The couple went to the city to do business with a cattle-driven cart. On their way to the town, they met three monks every day. The three monks ate sweet potatoes and fruit. Day in, day out, they tirelessly spread Buddhism. In winter, the three monks still slept in the open under a tree. Often they were so frozen that they were unable to go up the mountain to seek food. One day, the couple carried a lot of food on their cart. When they came to the place where the three monks stayed, they were surprised to see the three monks frozen under the tree, motionless. The couple swiftly brought some firewood and began to burn it by the monks. Very soon, the three monks began to move. The couple cooked a pot of gruel for them. Then, the three monks recited scriptures to the couple in return for their kindness. From then on, the people carried forward the tradition in the hope of getting blessed by the Buddha.

SAND PILING FESTIVAL

The festival falls on the 15th day of the first month of the Dai calendar (the 15th day of the tenth month in the Lunar Calendar). Early in the morning that day, the whole village would turn out to the river to collect sand and carry it to the courtyard of the village temple. They screen the sand and prepare lime and brisk for making sand pagoda. The biggest pagoda may be as tall as more than one meter, with bricks or abodes as the basement. The top of the pagoda is made of bamboo chips covered with painted paper. Around the pagoda is spread with fine sand while smaller pagodas are built by a mould. There are four clusters of small pagodas, with each cluster having 250 smaller ones, totaling 1,000. Some villages also plant small paper flags or fresh flowers or tree leaves around the sand pagodas. The whole thing is fenced up, with each corner having a bundle of banana leaves and a sugar cane with leaves to symbolize good harvest and happiness. Besides, some plates full of sweets, popped rice are tied to the fence as objects of offerings. Then the oil lamp in the Buddhist niches around the main pagoda is lit up and senior monks recite scriptures. The festival reaches its climax in the evening when the whole village turns out to converge to the temple, beating drums, singing and dancing. During the three-day festival, villagers all take their rice and dishes and eat around the pagodas built. The sand pagodas are cleared away on the afternoon of the third day. Children would look for bronze coins buried in the sand as a sign of luck.

Dai people regard pagoda as the Buddha and they deem sand is the cleanest and the presence of sand pagoda is the presence of divine. By worshiping the sand pagoda, they pray for the blessing by the Buddha. Apart from the sand piling festival, the Dai people also build sand pagodas during the Water Splashing Festival.

OFFERING TO PAGODA FESTIVAL

Offering to Pagoda is to make offerings to Pagoda with Buddha relics. Dai people regard Buddhist Pagoda as their patriarch. Dai people make small offerings every year and big offerings every three years. The small offering ceremony lasts two days and big offering ceremony lasts three days. Small offerings are made by villages and all villagers attend while big offerings are made by the whole prefecture and even disciples from Southeast Asian countries come to attend. According to Dai historical records, the Buddha died on June 15, 545. After cremation, the kings of eight countries took the bone relics home

◎ A Buddhist service in Ruili.

and enshrined them in their pagodas. When King Asoka began to spread Buddhism, he asked back all the bone relics and then distributed to 84,000 Buddhist temples all over the world. The earliest pagoda of the Dai area was built in the first half of January according to the Dai calendar and that day is fixed as a day for making offerings to Buddhist relics. On that day, all people, old and young, men and women, come from all directions to pay homage to the pagoda. Monks and Bhikhus all pay homage to pagodas at the next higher level. After kneeling down and kowtowing, they recite scriptures and pray, pour water onto the pagoda to wash it. Then the villagers would beat drums and gongs and elephant foot drums and danced. The festival ends with the letting off of firecrackers. During the festival, villagers all make their offerings. The money collected would be used to repair temples or sculpture Buddhist images. The village pagoda is repaired and serviced by the villagers; pagodas of the Zhou are repaired and serviced by several or even a dozen villages together. But after the 1950s, the local governments undertake to repair and service the pagodas.

There are quite a number of other festivals associated with Buddhism. They include Dan Xing, Dan Gang, Dan Chana, Dan Tan and Paga. Da Cha Na is to offer small pavilion built by villagers and it takes place in November of the Dai calendar. Now, they have changed the practice and offer paper elephants or horse to the Buddha. Some villagers offer live horses or elements to temples. Dan Tan is to offer scripture books on November 15, every year. On that day, all families would invite senior monks to recite scriptures or copy scriptures and then offer them to the Buddha. Paga is an irregular festival of the Dai people in Dehong area. It takes place several times a year. Paga is also known as Paladaga, meaning disciples of Buddhist family. People would offer to be disciples and pay money to buy titles, which are divided into three grades. For those who offer only one scripture book, the monk would grant the title of "Tan Mu"; for those who buy incense and present scripture paintings and books, clothes and quilts, meat and eggs to temples, the Temple master would grant the title of "Paga Chuang". Those who do so in three successive times would be invited as guests of a Buddhist service, they would be granted the title "Paga Ti". Whatever titles, they all feel greatly honored. Many disciples economize food and clothing and work for a whole life to realize the biggest aspirations of getting the title.

4. *Temples and Pagodas of Pali Buddhism in Yunnan*

(1) TEMPLES OF THERAVADA PALI BUDDHISM IN YUNNAN

A Buddhist temple in the Dai inhabited area is usually made up of a Buddha hall, a commandment hall and residential quarters for monks. Some have pagodas but most of them do not. Village temples do not have commandment hall. The layout is not as tight as those in the Han people inhabited areas, which features axle symmetry and enclosure on four sides. It is built with the going of the terrain, stressing naturalness and giving an impression of closeness. The walls around the temple complex are low and simple and some do not have walls at all. All the temples face east and the main ridges of neighboring structures are not allowed to be in the right angle. This is quite different from the Han Buddhist temples, which all face south.

The Buddha hall is the main structure, usually placed in the center. In front of it is the commandant hall and on the back are residences of monks. But the three are not in a central axle, with

© Manchunman Buddhist Temple.

the residences of monks either on the right or on the left of the central axle. There is no rule for the construction of the commandment hall. It is even placed in an out-of-the-way place. Some temples have front gates, but the gates do not face the main hall. Pagodas are built arbitrarily or even far away from villages. Ancillary structures include the drum room, corridor and scripture room, all laid out in a freewheeling fashion.

The Manlei Temple in Mengshu presents another style. The temple gates are at the foot of the mountain. It leads to the Buddha hall by a corridor with eight staircases. But the path does not connect with the Buddha Hall, which faces east. To the east of the Buddha Hall are residences of monks. There are no other structures around. The layout of the temples in Dehong Area is similar to that in the Xishuangbanna area, featuring naturalness, freedom and flexibility. But inside the temple complex are often built with water splashing pavilion and houses as temporary residences for disciples during festivals.

The Dadenghan Temple in Ruili does not have the front gates. A path leads to a corridor in the western direction and to northeast to the Buddha Hall. On the right of the Buddha Hall, there are rows of rooms for monks. On the left are big residential houses. On the northern end of the temple are five rows of smaller houses. In front of the Buddha Hall and the houses of monks is a water splashing pavilion. Both the Buddha Hall and the living houses for monks face east. But there are also houses facing south.

Commandment Hall (Octagonal Pavilion)

It is called "Bu sha" Hall in the Dai language or "octagonal pavilion" in the secular name. This is a forbidden area. It is a meeting place of masters to discuss major matters, recite scriptures, make confessions, and punish rule-violating monks. No people, monks or laymen, are allowed to enter and women are not even allowed to come near it.

Buddhist legend has it that "Bu Sha" is built on the model

of the golden filament hat of the Buddha. After the death of the Buddha, his disciples built such structures in Sri Lanka, India, Burma and Thailand. When Buddhism spread into Xishuangbanna, the image of the golden filament hat was also brought in with the pattra scriptures. Based on the design, people built a pavilion with eight angles. Dai people all call the Commandment Hall "Octagonal Pavilion", regardless of how many angles it has. All the temples above the central temple level have an Octagonal Pavilion. It is next only to the Buddha Hall in importance.

Jingzhen Octagonal Pavilion is a brilliant example of such structure. Built on a hill 16 kilometers from the Menghai County town, it is independent of any temple. It stands about 20 meters, with the basement in the shape of chinese character meaning "Asia" with 16 angles. The roof is very complicated and exquisite. Jingzhen Octagonal Pavilion was built in 1701, left over from the Qing Dynasty.

The houses for monks are of wood-and-fence structure. As Dai children would become monks at an early age, the houses are usually very big in order to accommodate as many monks as possible.

Jingzhen Octagonal Pavilion:

It is situated at Jingzhen, in the north of Mengzhe township, Menghai county. According to the records of the Dai nationality, the wooden pavilion was built in 1701 with a brick foundation. It is said that the monks built the pavilion in the shape of Sakyamuni's golden headgear. The foundation

◎ A Buddhist service in Ruili.

is two meters high, 8.25 meters long and 8.25 meters wide. The pavilion proper is 22 meters in height. On the top stands a silver umbrella rimmed with small bronze bells. On each of the eight eaves there are small bronze bells. When it breezes, the bells will ring in accordance. Novel in craft, light in structure and distinctive in style, it is one of the famous tourist attractions, especially for worshipers from at home and abroad.

The most famous temples of Theravada Buddhism in Yunnan are:

Mange Temple

Mange Temple is situated in Mange Village on the northern bank of Lancang River in the Yunjinghong Town of Jinghong city in Xishuangbanna. It is of central level temple. It is secularly called "Wa La Za Tan" in the Dai language. It is made up of the Buddha hall, the drum room, houses of monks, the commandment hall and the front gate pavilion. It was built in the year 840 by the Dai calendar (1478) with donations by villagers, monks and local officials. In the typical Dai style, it looks majestic and impressive, with 16 giant pillars measuring 40 cm. in diameter and 8 m. in height made of red tree of heaven, overlapped eaves

© Mange Temple.

and tiled roof. The whole structure of the temple is joined by mortises and tenons, and not a single nail is used, giving it a distinctive and resplendent appearance. On both ends of the hall are Buddha images in the sitting position, measuring about 4 meters high. The ceiling and the four walls are painted with peacocks, white elements and dragons, phoenixes and unicorns and other designs. The planning was organized by the senior monk Guba. The temple enjoys a high prestige in Xishuangbanna. Every close-door, open-door and water splashing festivals, thousands of pilgrims from at home and also from countries in Southeast Asia come here in steady streams to pay homage to it.

The temple was seriously damaged during the "Great Cultural Revolution" period. It was rebuilt by the Autonomous Zhou government in 1980 and listed it as a unit of cultural relics for priority protection.

Guangyun Temple

Situated in the Mengdong Street of the Lincang County town, the temple is no longer complete. It is of the blend style of the Dai and Han. The murals in the temple demonstrate the fusion of the Dai and Han cultures.

The main hall is 13 meters in depth. On the ceiling are

◎ Guangyun Temple.

painted with flowers and down below are human images. The windows and doors are carved with landscapes and other designs. With golden lacquer on the red background, it looks rich and elegant. On the column of the hall are two giant dragons carved in wood.

There are ten pieces of murals, with the biggest measuring about 3x 2 meters and the smallest measuring 1.2 x 2 meters. Among them two depict Buddhist stories and the other eight are landscape paintings, with an array of human beings.

The temple was built in 1828. The unique architectural art and exquisite murals are representatives of the Dai culture. In

1988, it was listed as key cultural relics for protection.

Guanmian Temple

Situated on the outskirts of Gengma County in Lincang Prefecture, it is a temple with the highest ranking in the prefecture. It is called "Nazatan Tansi" in the Dai language. It used to be a place where the local Tusi and family to pay homage. The temple was rebuilt twice in the reign of emperors Xian Feng and Guang Xu.

Puti Temple

It is in the Zhennan Street of Mangshi Town of Luxi City. It was first built at the beginning of the Qing Dynasty. It is called "Zai Xiang" in the Dai language, meaning "precious stone temple". The temple has a vast courtyard, occupying an area of 3,100 square meters. The Buddha Hall is in the center, facing east. In front of the hall, there are two beautifully decorated pavilions, one on the right side and the other on the left, with a small dual eaves water splashing pavilion in between them. The Buddha Hall is of special shape, with triple eaves and rows of columns

Bajie Temple - General Temple of Xishuangbanna

The main temple is situated in the Manlongkuan Village in Jinghong City, capital of the Xishuangbanna Dai Autonomous Zhou. The earliest Buddhist temple in the area, the temple used to be very small and dilapidated. In the 1980s, with the support of the local government, it was rebuilt by local Buddhists and with the aid from the neighboring Thailand and Burma. Thailand presented a lucky Buddhist statue, which is now enshrined in the temple. Bajie Temple is the main temple in the Xishuangbanna area, responsible for the Buddhist affairs of the whole autonomous Zhou (prefecture). The Xishuangbanna Buddhism Institute is

◎ General Temple .

situated there to train Pali Buddhists. Graduates from the institute have been sent to Burma, Sri Lanka and other countries for further study. The temple has a Buddha Hall, a Bhiksu commandment hall and other halls and houses.

(2) BUDDHIST PAGODAS

Pagodas are places for enshrining the teeth, hair, footprints, sculptures and statues of the Buddha. Buddhists in the Dai inhabited areas regard pagoda as the incarnation of the Buddha and that is why pagodas are usually higher than temples. The Dai pagodas are beautifully built to cater to various Buddhist activities. There are pagodas, which were built at the instructions of Sakyamuni, such as Zhuangmo Pagoda and Zhuangdong Pagoda; there are also pagodas where Sakyamuni left relics, such as Manfeilong Pagoda. Pagodas are seen everywhere in the areas inhabited by Dai people. In Xishuangbanna alone, there are more than 100 pagodas.

Pagodas are built not necessarily in temples, because pagodas are built before temples. But in main temples, pagodas and temples are built at the same time. There are pagodas but not necessarily temples. But when a pagoda is built, there must be a temple. The pagodas and temples are repaired and serviced by villages. Usually one pagoda is maintained by a number of Buddhist temples and villages. In Menglong, there are 16 pagodas, which are maintained by 59 temples and 71 villages.

A pagoda is usually of brick structure, small and simple. It is made up the basement, the body and the top. The basement is mostly square in shape or in the shape of multiple angles or in oval. The body of the pagoda is thick at the bottom and becomes thinner with the rise of the height, just like a spring bamboo shoot. The top of the pagoda is made up of the lotus seat, top rail, wheel, umbrella, precious bottle and pearl. Most of the tops are covered with layer upon layer of umbrellas, giving a strong decorative effect. The top is made of bronze, gilded or plastered with gold. The most famous pagodas include the following:

Manfeilong Pagoda:

It is a group of the most famous pagodas in Yunnan. Standing at the top of the Manfeilong Hill, it was built in 1204. There are altogether nine white bamboo shoot- like structures, laid out in the shape of a lotus flower. The pagoda in the center is the highest, with 16 meters. The basement is round, with eight niches facing eight directions and each niche has a Buddhist statue, with a number of small Buddha images flanking the bigger one. In the

◎ Manfeilong pagoda.

front of the niches are decorated with dragon and phoenix and peacock designs. Facing the eight niches are eight smaller pagodas, in the same shape as the central pagoda.

Jiele Golden Pagoda

In the Jiele Village of Ruili City of Dehong, the pagoda was said to be built on a place where Buddhist bones, which are varied in color and size and shine at night, were found. It is composed of 17 ring-shaped pagodas. The major pagoda stands 36 meters, surrounded by 16 satellite pagodas that are smaller in size and shorter in height. The main pagoda was damaged in 1966 and rebuilt in April 1983. In 1984, 16 smaller pagodas were rebuilt.

Yunyan Pagoda

This is also a group of pagodas in the Maoluchang of Yunyan village in Yingjiang County. It has 41 pagodas, one main pagoda and 40 satellite pagodas. The main pagoda stands 20 meters. It is of solid brick structure, with a five-layer square basement. On the four sides of the first layer are 28 small pagodas. On the second through fourth layers, each platform has s small pagoda on the four corners. The main pagoda stands on the top layer. It is in the shape of a bell.

CHAPTER V
BUDDHISM IN CONTEMPORARY CHINA

1. Buddhism and Contemporary China

Following the founding of the People's Republic of China and before the Constitution was promulgated, China published a "Common Program of the Chinese People's Political Consultative Conference". Article 5 of the common program stipulates: "The people of the People's Republic of China enjoy the freedom of thinking, speech, publishing, assembly, association, communications, person, residence, movement, religious beliefs and demonstration and parade."

This enlightening policy toward religions played a positive

role in encouraging many religious leaders to join the anti-imperialist and anti-feudal democratic revolutionary movement and shared weal and woe with the Communist Party of China.

In 1952, Chairman Mao Zedong said in his meeting with a Tibetan delegation: "The Communist Party of China adopts a policy of protecting religions. All believers and non-believers, believers of this kind or that kind of religion, are all brought under protection and their beliefs are respected. We follow this policy of protection today and so shall we in the future." His speech was a summation of the correct policy of the Chinese Communist Party over the previous scores of years and became a guideline for handling religious affairs at the beginning of the founding of the People's Republic and served as a basis for the article about the freedom of religion in the Constitution later on.

In September 1954, the First National People's Congress adopted the Constitution. Article 88 of the Constitution stipulates: "The citizens of the People's Republic of China enjoy the freedom of religion". The codification of this provision was confirmed by the fundamental law of the state.

In 1957, Mao Zedong made his famous speech, saying that "we cannot eliminate religions by administrative orders; we cannot coerce people not to believe in religion. We cannot coerce people to give up idealism. Neither can we coerce people to believe in Marxism."

In 1966-1976, when the Great Cultural Revolution took place, the Buddhist Association of China was forced to cease functioning. Buddhist organizations paralyzed. Temples were damaged.

When the Great Cultural Revolution ended in 1976, governments at all levels and Buddhist circles began to restore the religious policy and rebuild temples damaged. In the 20-30 years after that, thanks to the support of the government, Buddhism began to develop rapidly, not only in terms of the rebuilding of temples but also in Buddhist affairs, education, culture and foreign exchanges, changes that are rare for several hundred years. At the same time, the Buddhist Association of China has advanced a new road of development in contemporary China that is in keeping with the development of the contemporary society. Buddhists in China must adhere to the authentic world outlook that everything arises from the immateriality of the nature of all things and the outlook on life that the Buddhists must be selfless and ready to deliver all human beings tirelessly, and the moral principle of doing no evils but doing good for all people. At the same time, Buddhists should carry forward the fine traditions in philosophy, literature and arts, ethics and morality, natural sciences and life sciences so as to make contributions to the development of the civilization. Besides, Buddhists must carry forward the spirit of loving their country and loving their religion and actively respond to the calls by the government to keep pace with the times so as to become a force that propels the society forward.

It is exactly because of the good relations between the government and religious circles and the correct policy toward religion that Buddhism has gained vigorous development in contemporary China, a good situation that has been rare for hundreds of years.

2. *Buddhist Association of China*

The Buddhist Association of China is an organization of Buddhism believers of all nationalities. The basic situation of the organizations can be found in the General Principles of the Constitution of the Buddhist Association of China adopted at its 7th Congress in September 2002.

Article 1 of Chapter One fixes the English name of the association as THE BUDDHIST ASSOCIATION OF CHINA (BAC for short).

Article 2 states that the association is a patriotic group and religious affairs organization of Buddhism believers of all nationalities in the country. Its main purpose is to assist the people's government in implementing the policy of religious freedom, protect the lawful rights and interests of Buddhists, carry forward the Buddhist doctrines, run Buddhist undertakings, carry forward the fine traditions of Buddhism, strengthen the building of Buddhism, hold high the banner of loving the country and loving Buddhism to unite Buddhists of all nationalities of the country, advocate for Buddhist doctrines in the human world, take an active part in the building of material and spiritual civilization, open up new ground and make new innovations, keep pace with the times, uphold the dignity of prominent figures, bring happiness and welfare to the people and make contributions to the reunification of the motherland and to world peace.

Article 3 provides the tasks of the association. It states:

(1) To safeguard the right of religious freedom of Buddhism believers and the lawful rights and interests of Buddhist activity sites, cultural and educational organizations and Buddhist service undertakings; keep a close tie with Buddhists of all nationalities, carry out in-depth investigations and study, reflect situation as it is, and implement the religious policies and put forward recommendations and proposals with departments concerned;

(2) To study the constitution and related laws, regulations and policies, heighten the patriotic consciousness of Buddhism believers and self consciousness compatible with the socialist society and love the country, love Buddhism and observe discipline and law.

(3) To support local chapters of the association in carrying out religious activities and providing guidance and oversight over the religious affairs in various provinces, autonomous regions

and municipalities. All chapters of the association, Buddhist temples, Buddhist institutions and other Buddhist organizations shall implement the resolutions and decisions of the Association.

(4) To supervise Buddhist temples in their own building and management, strictly observe Buddhist rules and commandments, foster a good style of learning and carry out normal Buddhist services, formulate rules and regulations and implementation rules for temples and for Buddhist regimes.

To provide guidance and see to it that lay Buddhist groups to improve their organizations, systems, strengthen unity and coordinate their steps, study hard and strengthen self cultivation, safeguard the three treasures (Buddha, Dharma, and sangha), observe discipline and law and serve the social public.

(5) To run Buddhist education cause to train Buddhists excelled in the four varga (groups, or orders), i. e. bhiksu, bhiksuni, upasaka and upasika (monks, nuns, male and female devotees), raise the general quality of Buddhists, carry out Buddhist cultural and academic studies, compile and print and distribute Buddhist books and magazines and protect Buddhist relics and historical sites.

(6) To encourage Buddhism believers to work hard in their respective posts and run all kinds of self-supporting services that

◎ Master Guo Ying, the first president of the Chinese Buddhist Association.

conform to the Buddhist rules, support and participate in the development public welfare undertakings to benefit the society and interest groups.

(7) To carry out friendly exchanges with Buddhists among Taiwan, Hong Kong and Macao compatriots and overseas Chinese to enhance mutual understanding, strengthen unity and cooperation and promote the reunification of the motherland and the development of Buddhism

(8) To carry out exchange and cooperation with Buddhist organizations of other countries and friendly international Buddhist organizations, international religious peace organizations and promote cultural exchange with foreign Buddhist organizations and promote world peace.

Article 4 provides that the association is headquartered in Beijing.

The Buddhist Association of China was founded in 1953

upon the sponsorship of Master Xu Yun, Master Sherab Gyamtso, Master Yuan Ying and Zhao Puchu. During the half century, the association has held seven national congresses. The national congress of September 16-20, 2002 was the most ceremonious. At the congress, quite a number of vigorous middle-aged and young monks were elected into the leading body in addition to Mater Sheng Hui and Master Xue Cheng. It was regarded to have opened up a new period of historical development. The young Buddhists could live more in harmony with the modern society and Buddhism would be brought into breadth and depth.

3. Contemporary Buddhist Figures

SHERAB GYAMTSO (SHES RAB RGYA MTSHO)

Sherab Gyamtso (1883-1968) was a grand master of Tibetan Buddhism. He was born in a Tibetan family in Xunhua County, Qinghai Province. He began to study Buddhist doctrines from early childhood. He studied at the Jilei Temple in his hometown,

© Sherab Gyamtso.

the Bla-bran monastery in Gansu and Jokhang monastery. Thanks to his strenuous efforts, he has became a grand scholar in the Tibetan area. In 1916, he got the highest degree of Tibetan Buddhism and in 1918-1932, at the invitation of 13th Dalai Lama, he began to compile Tibetan "Collection of Sugata" and

"Tripitaka-Bak-gyur". In 1936, the Kuomintang government invited him to be a lecturer at five major universities. In 1937, he left Tibet for Nanjing via India, beginning his journey of spreading Tibetan culture and safeguarding national unity. After the founding of the People's Republic of China, he stayed in the Chinese mainland. He served as a vice-governor of Qinghai Province, and standing committee member of the National Committee of the Chinese People's Political Consultative Conference (CPPCC). His main job was the president of the Buddhist Association of China and president of China Buddhism Institute. He served as the first, second and third presidents of the Buddhist Association of China. He made great contributions to safeguarding national unity and carrying forward traditional culture. He led a number of delegations to Burma, Nepal and India.

BAINQEN ERDINI QOIGYI GYAINCAIN

Bainqen Erdini Qoigyi Gyaincain (1938-1989), native (Tibetan) of Xunhua, Qinghai Province. With a secular name of Qoinbo Cedan, he was born into a Tibetan peasant family in Wendu township, Xunhua County, of Qinghai Province, on February 3, 1938.

© Bainqen erdini Qoigyi Gyaincain.

After the death of the ninth Panchen Lama on December 1, 1938, the Panchen Kampo Lija, the highest administrative committee headed by the Panchen Lama, chose in 1941 the three-year-old Goinbo Cedan as the incarnation of the Ninth Panchen Lama according to the established religious procedures and practices.

On June 3, 1949, Li Zongren, acting president of the Nationalist Government, issued an order approving Goinbo Cenda as the reincarnated child of the Ninth Panchen Lama and said that the ceremony of drawing lots from a gold urn could be dispensed with.

On August 10 of the same year, an installation ceremony was held at the Gumbum Monastery in Qinghai Province. He was given the name "Luosang Cilie Lunzhu Qoiyyi Gyaincian".

Thus, Qoigyi Gyaincain officially assumed the status and

power of all previous Panchen Lamas. He followed the teacher of the Ninth Panchen Lama to study Buddhist scriptures. But as the teacher was too old, Lama Xiya acted as his instructor.

Immediately after the liberation of Xining, capital of Qinghai Province, 1949, the 10th Panchen Lama sent emissaries to make contact with the Communist Party of China. When the People's Republic of China was founded on October 1, he immediately cabled Chairman Mao Zedong and commander-in-chief Zhu De pledging his support for the CPC and the people's government and expressing his wish for the early liberation of Tibet and for making contributions to the unification of the country. On April 27, 1951, he led a 45-member delegation of the Kampo Lija to Beijing to participate in the talks with the central government on the peaceful liberation of Tibet. On May 23, the same year, the central government and Tibetan local government signed an agreement on the peaceful liberation of Tibet. On May 29, Panchen Lama issued a statement, expressing his support to the signing of the agreement. The following day, the 14th Dalai Lama expressed willingness for unity. In September 1954, Panchen Lama was elected a member of the Standing Committee of the National People's Congress (NPC) in Beijing. In December the same year, he was elected vice-chairman of the CPPCC National Committee. He was then 16 years old. From then on, he was not only a political leader of Tibet but also a leader of the state. In April 1956, the preparatory committee for the establishment of Tibet Autonomous Region was set up and he served as the first vice-chairman member and acting chairman. In November 1956, at the invitation of the Indian government, he went to India to participate in the activities marking the 2500th anniversary of the death of Sakyamuni and paid a friendly visit to India. He was given an honorary doctor's degree by the Benares Buddhist University.

In July 1979, Panchen Lama was elected vice-chairman of the 5th CPPCC National Committee. In 1980, he was elected vice-chairman of the NPC Standing Committee. In the ten years that followed, he worked hard and made great contributions to the development of Tibet and the restoration and development of Tibetan Buddhism. He paid special attention to Buddhism education. With his support, an advanced college of Tibetan Buddhism was opened in Beijing in 1987 and he served as the president.

In January 1989, Panchen left Beijing to Tibet to participate in the eye-opening ceremony for the joint burial of 5th-9th Panchen Lamas. At 8:35 am, January 28, he passed away with a sudden heart attack. He was then 51 years old.

LAY BUDDHIST ZHAO PUCHU

Zhao Puchu was born in 1907 in Taihu County, Anhui Province. In his early years, he studied at Dongwu University of Suzhou City. After 1928, he served as secretary of Shanghai-based Jiangsu-Zhejiang Buddhist Union, secretary of Shanghai Buddhist Association and head of the "Buddhism Purification Service". After 1938, he was a council member of the Shanghai Salvation Association of Shanghai Cultural Circles and Secretary of the China Buddhism Society. He was also a major sponsor for several social welfare institutions and took charge of refugee reception during the War of Resistance against Japan.

After 1953 he served as vice-chairman and secretary-general of the China Buddhist Association, council member of the Chinese Writers Association, and vice-president of the Sino-Japan Friendship Association.

After 1980, he served as President of the China Buddhism Association, president of the China Buddhism Institute, advisor to the China Advanced Tibetan Buddhism College, chairman of the China Religious Committee for Peace and vice-president of the China Calligraphic Association.

◎ Lay Buddhist Zhao Puchu.

He was member of the first through third CPPCC National Committees, member of the Standing Committees of Fourth and Fifth CPPCC National Committees, vice-chairman of 6th to 8th CPPCC national Committees, and a deputy to the 1st to 5th National People's Congresses.

Zhao Puchu was a leading member of China's Buddhism after the founding of the People's Republic of China. For half a century, he explored ways of how to adapt Buddhism to the contemporary Chinese society and how to achieve unity of loving the country and loving Buddhism and how to serve modern society. He made outstanding contributions to the implementation of the freedom of religion policy, to the improvement of the Buddhism systems and to foreign exchanges with other countries. He was not only a good friend of the CPC and the Chinese government but also an esteemed Buddhist leader.

Zhao was also a respected social activist, a poet and a writer. He died on May 21, 2000 at the age of 93.

In his late years, he showed great concern for the cause of charity, often raising relief funds for victims of natural disasters. He donated all his royalties and life-long savings to the cause of charity. He left his will that he would contribute his remains to medical colleges. He also left a short poem in his will:

It is a pleasure to live, but it is no pity to die,
Flowers bloom and fade, water flows ceaselessly;
Whatever I have will rest in peace together with me,
Everything will go with the wind,
And there should be no trouble to seek me.

SONGLIE AGAMUNI

Songlie Agamuni (1899-1974) was a senior monk of Buddhism in areas inhabited by the Dai people, equivalent to the king of monks and grand master of Buddhism. Of Dai nationality, Agamuni was a senior monk of the Run Section of Southern Buddhism, often called by the people as "Guba Meng".

He became a "pa" (novice) in 1913 and rose to the position as a "du" (bhiksu) in 1923 and received completed commandments in 1936 to become "gu ba" (presbyter) and was promoted to "sha mi" (General presbyter). In 1956, he was promoted to Songlie Amingmuni (grand presbyter) under the sponsorship of the Chinese Buddhist Association.

Songlie Agamuni loved the country and loved Buddhism. He served as a member of the CPPCC National Committee, vice-president of the Buddhist Association of China, president of the Yunnan chapter of the Buddhist Association of China and president of the Buddhist Association of the Xishuangbanna Dai Autonomous Zhou. In 1956, at the invitation of the Burmese government and the Burmese Buddhist Association, he led a Chinese Buddhist

◎ Songlie Agamuni.

delegation for the 2500th anniversary of the death of Sakyamuni and the closing ceremony of the Sixth Assembly. During his stay in Burma, he met the Burmese government leaders. His delegation took the Buddhist teeth back to Yunnan. In 1960, he went to Burma again with the then Premier Zhou Enlai for the celebrations of the Independence Day of Burma.

WUBINYA WINSA

Wubinya Winsa is a native of Ruili County, Hongzhou. In 1949, he was the fifth abbot of the Xiansha Temple of Ruili County. In 1958-1982, he was spreading Buddhism in Burma. He returned in 1983 and continued his post as the abbot at Hansa Temple in Ruili and served as president of the Ruili Buddhist Association, council member of the Buddhist Association of China and member of the CPPCC National Committee.

YI CHENG, MASTER OF LAW

With the secular name as Gu Rongsheng, Yi Cheng is a native of Hubei Province. He became a monk in June 1949, following the contemporary Chinese Guru of the Chan Sect Monk Xu Yun. After the death of Monk Xu Yun, he carried forward the fine style of Buddhism. Living in Juyun Mountain, he devoted

◎ Master Yi Cheng.

his life to the spread of the Chan Sect of Buddhism. His temple owns more than 200 hectares of mountain forests, all attended by his monks.

Yi Cheng is good at calligraphy and loves writing poems. He enjoys a high reputation in the Chinese Buddhist circles.

Yi Cheng is now president of the Jiangxi Provincial Buddhist Association, president of the Buddhist Association of China and vice-chairman of the CPPCC Jiangxi Provincial Committee and member of the Standing Committee of the CPPCC National Committee.

© Master Sheng Hui, vice-president of the Chinese Buddhist Association.

SHENG HUI, MASTER OF LAW

Sheng Hui has the secular name of Sheng Qinghui. He was born in 1951 in Xiangtan, Hunan Province. In 1981, he received complete commandments and in the following year, he was enrolled in the China Buddhism Institute. In 1989, he finished the study as a postgraduate and became a teacher in the institute. Then, he was sent to Jiuhua Mountain to train temple management personnel for the country. After he became vice-president of the Buddhist Association of China in 1993, he attended many international conferences, especially the world human rights conference in Geneva. He briefed the Geneva conference on the human rights conditions in China, winning extensive approval.

Sheng Hui is now executive vice-president of the Buddhist Association of China. Besides, he is also the Abbot of the South Putuo Temple in Xiamen, Fujian Province, president of the Hunan Provincial Buddhist Association, Abbot of the Lushan Temple in Changsha, Abbot of the Beijing Lingguang Temple and member of the Standing Committee of the CPPCC National Committee.

XUE CHENG, MASTER OF LAW

Xue Cheng, with the secular name as Fu Ruilin, was born on August 19, 1966 in Xianyou County, Fujian Province. He became a monk in his childhood. In 1989, he graduated from the China Buddhism Institute and went on to pursue further study as a postgraduate. In 1999, he served as Abbot of the Guanghua Temple in Putian City, Fujian Province. He was then only 24, the youngest Abbot in the country. Xue Cheng sets great store by the styles of study and the law. He held a number of services to pass on Bhiksu commandments.

Xue Cheng is not only knowledgeable but also shows concern for world peace and environmental protection and other major problems in human civilization. He published a number

◎ Master Xue Cheng, vice-president and secreatary-general of the Chinese Buddhist Association.

of articles that were well received. In 2003, Xue Cheng was elected vice-president and secretary general of the Buddhist Association of China at its 7th national congress to become the youngest Buddhism leader in China. He is now a member of the CPPCC National Committee.

4. Buddhism Ceremonies

THE FOUR DIVISIONS OF DISCIPLES AND BUDDHIST TEMPLES

The believers of the Han-language Buddhism are mostly people of the Han nationality. Many people believe in Buddhism but do not go through any initiation ceremonies. Such Buddhists make up the overwhelming majority. Only a small part of Buddhists have gone through the ceremony which makes the recipient an upasaka or upasika and accepted the five commandments. They are formal Buddhists.

The three surrenders, Trisarana, or Sarana-gamana, are surrender to the Buddha, the law, the ecclesia, known as three precious ones. The Buddha refers to Sakyamuni and all other Buddhas; the law refers to the teachings and all theories of Buddhism. Monks refer to all who have given up their secular life. Having surrendered to the Buddha, the law and the ecclesia, one has become a disciple of Buddhism. Five commandments are the first five of the ten commandments against killing, stealing, adultery, lying, and intoxicating liquor.

Kulapati or lay Buddhist is a householder who practises Buddhism at home without becoming a monk. Male kulapati is called upasaka, meaning practising Buddhism at home; female kulapati is called upasoka. These are callings corresponding to monks, nuns, and male and female devotees. They are collectively known as the four divisions of disciples.

Chinese Buddhists practise Buddhim either at home or in temples. Those who practise Buddhism at home also attend major services and other festive activities in temples.

The layout of a temple of the Han-language Buddhism is very strict. It takes the layout of traditional Chinese palace

◎ "Hm-ha generals" at Fahua Temple in Hangzhou.

◎ Dhrtarastra, king for protecting the land territory.

◎ Virudhaka, capable of making people to have a kind heart.

architecture. It usually has a group of courtyards and halls set on the north-south axis with side rooms flanking symmetrically on each side.

The entrance or introductory part of the temple is called Mountain Gate (Shan Men), guarded by two angels, one with closed mouth as if producing the sound (hem) and the other with open mouth, as if producing the sound (ha), secularly known as "hem-ha generals).

After entering the gate there is the first courtyard, also called forecourt. Bell Tower and Drum Towers are two-storied

◎ Virupaksa, meaning it is capable of feeling the life of human beings with a broad vision.

◎ Dhanada, meaning great virtue and happiness, known the world over.

structures, set symmetrically on each side of the yard. In the past times, bells and drums were used as a time alert. Nowadays they no longer have any function like that. In small temples, they were replaced by pavilions. There is a path in the middle leading to the Heavenly Kings Hall (Tian Wang Dian or Devaraja Hall), the first main hall on the axis. In this hall, a smiling Maitreya (known as smiling Buddha) is set on the middle altar. Four fierce-looking Heavenly Kings or four Deva-Kings (warrior guardians) stand in two groups on each side. One is known as Dhrtarastra, meaning a king for protecting the land territory. With a sword in the left hand and a spear in the right hand, the Deva King has a white body. The second is known as Virudhaka, meaning it is capable of making people to have a kind heart. With a bluish body, it holds a sword in hand. The third is known as Virupaksa, meaning it is capable of feeling the life of human beings with a broad vision. With a reddish body, it holds a long spear in the left hand and a red rope in the right. The fourth is known as Dhanada, meaning great virtue and happiness, known the world over. Holding a mini-stupa in the left hand and a long spear in the right hand, it stamps on a yaksa (one of the eight classes of supernatural beings) under one of his feet. The four Deva Kings are originally Indian but they are localized in China. The things in hands have also changed. In the hands of Virudhaka is the sword; while Dhrtarastra holds a Pipa (A Chinese musical string instrument); Dhanada holds an umbrella while Virupaksa holds a snake. Behind the smiling Buddha is Skanda holding a vajra , a god for protecting the law.

Behind the Heavenly Kings Hall is the second courtyard, the principal part of the temple which includes the Main Buddha Hall and several flanking rooms. The Main Buddha Hall stands on a high terrace or foundation with marble balustrades. The hall is variably named Daxiongbaodian. A common case is the

Buddha trinity (the trinity of the three ages) including the Buddha of the Present, Sakyamuni, the Buddha of the Past, Kasyapa (Jiayefo in Chinese Pinyin) and the Buddha of the Future, Maitreya or another trinity often found in Chan temples of Sakyamuni, Amitabha (Emituofo) and Bhaisajyaguru (Yaoshifo, the God of Medicine). The case varies with different Buddhist schools and periods in which the temples were built.

A huge bronze incense burner or Ding - a kind of bronze cooking vessel is used for religious or ritual ceremonies and is found in front of the Main Buddha Hall for people to burn incense. Side rooms in this courtyard house other Buddhas or reputed dignitaries.

Behind the Main Buddha Hall is another courtyard with more halls serving other purposes. A library hall, often a two-storied tower in which Buddhist sutras, scriptures, and books are kept is called Cang Jing Ge (Sutra Keeping Tower or Sutra Hall). It is usually found at the rear part of the courtyard. Living residences or quarters are set at the corner of the rear part for monks and pupils.

Some ancient temples also have stupas or pagodas, such as the Bailin Temple in Hebei Province and Famen Temple in Shaanxi Province.

Eye-opening ceremony for new Buddha statues

An eye-opening ceremony is held to consecrate a new place for enshrining the Buddha or a new Buddha statue. It is said that the ceremony may enable a wooden image of the Buddha to have a sharp vision and all believers wish to have their aspirations and behavior to be seen by the Buddha. As the Buddha image is made of wood, it needs repairing very often and each repair will be followed by an eye-opening ceremony. When an eye-opening ceremony is held, the temple would invite all monks of the temple and temples elsewhere to participate. Sometimes the number of attendants may come to hundreds of thousands. While the monks are reciting Buddhist sutras, the

◎ Statue of Skanda.

◎ Eye-opening ceremony for the open-air bronze statue of Avalokitesvara on Mount Putuo on October 30, 1997.

master of the law uses a Chinese writing brush to brush the eyes and draw the eyeballs of the Buddha image from a distance.

CEREMONY FOR PROMOTION TO ABBOT

Each Buddhist temple has an abbot, the most authoritative monk to take charge all affairs of the temple. The traditional practice is to have the abbot recommended by all monks of a temple. When the nomination is fixed, a grand ceremony is held. The new abbot would enter the temple from the Shan Men (the front gate) into every hall while reciting his sutras. A prestigious

© Promotion ceremony for Master Sheng Hui.

master of the law is invited to send the abbot to his new post. On September 6, 2003, vice-president Sheng Hui was made the abbot of the Lingguang Temple in Beijing and he was set to the seat by Yi Cheng, the master of the law and president of the Buddhist Association of China. On September 8, 2003, master of the law Yi Cheng was made the abbot of Fayuan Temple in Beijing and he was sent to the seat by Fo Yuan of the Dajue Temple of the Chan Sect in Yunmen, Guangdong Province. Thousands of people attended the ceremony.

COMMANDMENT PASSING CEREMONY

A person must accept the commandments to become a monk. There are two grades of commandments or prohibitions, of which ten commandments or complete commandments for monks; five and eight commandments for the laity; and there are heretical rules and correct rules; and numerous other pairs in addition to the bhiksu commandments which have more than 200 rules and bhiksuni commandments that have more than 400 rules. To become a monk, one has to accept three types of commandments, namely, the ten commandments of the sramanera, the nun's '500 rules' and the eight commanding respects

◎ Guanghua Temple in Putian, Fujian Province, held a service of passing on bhik?u commandments on March 27-April 28, 2003.

◎ A service of passing on bhiksu commandments at Aidao Temple in Chengdu.

for monks and bodhisattva commandments. bhiksu and bhiksuni commandments are the most important. Only those who want to become monks can accept these commandments. In the past, it took more than 40 days to pass on the commandments. But in recent years, the time has been shortened. Still, it is a hard and unforgettable experience. In the past, a bhiksu or bhiksuni used to have nine or three scars burned by incense on the head to express his or her determination to be loyal to Buddhism. But in the 1980s, the Buddhist Association of China issued a circular to all Buddhists, demanding that temples cancel such practice. But there are also a small number of people who do so, especially in Taiwan. A bhiksu or bhiksuni will get a document to certify the initialization. The certificate bears the name of the person who accepted the commandments, his Buddhist name given, his secular name, age and the temple where he or she accepted the commandments, date of accepting the commandments and the Buddhist names of three masters of the law and seven witnesses. Now, in China, such commandment ceremonies have to be put on the record with the Buddhist Association of China, which will send people to issue the certificates.

BUDDHA BATHING FESTIVAL

Buddha bathing festival is a grand service to mark the birth anniversary of Sakyamuni. But there are different interpretations about the birth of Sakyamuni among Han-language, Tibetan and Southern Buddhism. The water splashing festival held in Yunnan on April 5 every year is a Buddha bathing festival of the Southern Buddhism. But for the Han-language Buddhism, the date falls on the eighth day of the fourth month of the lunar calendar, usually a day in May. On this day, Buddhism believers all converge to temples to recite Buddhist scriptures before washing the statue

◎ Service for releasing captive animals and living things at Guangji Temple, Beijing.

of child Sakyamuni, which stands with one hand pointing up to the sky and the other hand pointing down to the earth. In some places, the statue is nude or with only a fig around the waist. The child Buddha image stands in a water basin, covered by a shed woven with tree branches and flowers. Buddhism believers use a small ladle to pour water from head down.

The festival is originated in a legend, which says that when the Buddha was born, a dragon spewed water from the sky to wash the Buddha. Buddhist followers regard the water used to wash the statue as sacred water and after washing the statue, the believers also pour a ladle of water onto themselves. The festival is accompanied by ceremonies for releasing animals in captivity and other living things, such as birds, fish and turtle.

FEEDING ULKA-MUKHA (FESTIVAL OF HUNGRY GHOSTS)

Feeding hungry ghosts is a wide-spread Buddhist service in China. "Ulka-mukha" (flaming mouth) is represented in the Buddhist sutras as a hungry ghost (preta). In addition to a very thin appearance, it has a throat that is no bigger than needles, and a mouth that spits out flame. It is originated in the Yogacara Ulka-mukha Preta Sutra, which runs up to more than 18,000 words, with more than 130 pictures, covering poems and verses.

◎ Feeding Ulka-mukha at Guangji Temple in Beijing.

Feeding hungry ghosts is a major Buddhist service in temples. The religious meaning is to deliver the soul of the dead. So when a person dies, the family would invite monks to perform the service of feeding hungry ghosts so that the dead would go to the western paradise.

In feeding hungry ghosts, a ghost image is hung behind the main seat for the ghost feeding monk. In front is another long table on which incenses, candles and ritual instruments are placed and around the table are sitting other monks. For some services of larger scale, there are three main seats, three tables and three pendants. In the past, rich families used to invite monks from two different temples to perform the service in rivalry.

Another kind of hungry ghost feeding service is done not for any particular family but for many ghosts. It is called the Day of the Buddha's Rejoicing or Ullambana Festival or ghost festival secularly. It is a tradition to recite scriptures to deliver the soul of the dead. Any one may contribute some money to have a niche for his dead relatives.

WATER-AND-LAND SERVICE

It is a Buddhism service for delivering dead souls in water and on land. Activities include recital of Buddhist scriptures and offering of food and presents. It is a major Buddhist service in

◎ Water-and-land service at Guanghua Temple.

China. At present, the service is performed in both inner and outer altars, with the inner altar as the main service site. In the middle of the altar are placed the statues of Vairocana, Sakyamuni and Amitabha and tables of offerings and a platform for placing ritual instruments.

The water-and-land service is designed to save all beings in the life cycle and bring benefit to living beings. It is regarded as having a boundless merit and virtue.

INCARNATION OF LIVING BUDDHA

The reincarnation system (tulku), a distinguishing characteristic of Tibetan Buddhism, is based the theory that Buddha's soul never vanishes, but reincarnates in succession to lead his followers and to accomplish his mission. One of the first reincarnations among the Buddhist monks in Tibet is Karma Pakshi. In 1193, before Dusum Chenpa, a religious leader, the first Karmapa of the Karma Kagyu tradition of Tibetan Buddhism, passed away. Before he died, he told his disciples that he would return as a reincarnated being. His disciples soon led a search for his infant reincarnation in accordance with his will. Several years later, Karma Pakshi turned out as the first reincarnation in Tibet and trained to be Karma Kagyu leader. After Karma Pakshi's reincarnation, the reincarnation system was adopted by other sects gradually to keep a consistent religious leadership. By applying the system, heirs for hundreds of Gyalwas (Living Buddhas) were selected, among whom the Dalai Lama and the Panchen Lama are the most prestigious. The Yellow Hat sect also applied Gelugpa tradition of Tibetan Buddhism to hand down the titles conferred on the third Dalai Lama and the fourth Panchen Lama to keep their established religious and secular title and power. By the end of the Qing Dynasty there were 160 high lamas registered with the Board for Mongolian and Tibetan Affairs, each applying the reincarnation system to identify their next successors.

Religious methods and rituals are used to identify a reincarnation of a late high lama. A search party headed by another high lama begins the search. After a religious retreat, lamas, dispatched in disguise, scour Tibet for special signs: new mothers who had unusual dreams, children who have special knowledge without being taught, and special physical traits, such as big ear lobes. The lamas refer to oracles, portents, dreams and the late lama's prophesy in order to aid them in their search. Some lamas are sent to Lhamo Latso, the Oracle Lake, to look for prophetic visions to help locate the reincarnation.

Usually, dozens of candidates are sought. They will be tested with the late lama's possessions; those who have amazing knowledge in identifying their predecessor's belongings win and become the final candidates. Since the search could be easily manipulated and dispute occurs (as in the case of the sixth Dalai Lama), Emperor Qian Long of the Qing Dynasty decided to use a golden urn lottery as a divination to eliminate false candidates. The names and birth dates of the final candidates are written on ivory lots, wrapped up and sealed in the urn. Religious rituals are held before the lot drawing. After holding the lottery in the Jokhang Temple, a new religious leader is soon installed if the procedure has been verified by the central government.

There are the following established procedures and practices of the reincarnation of living Buddha:

1. Prior to the death of a living Buddha, he would leave a will, telling where his rebirth would take place and what the characteristics of the locality are. If no will is left, the monks of the temple would get enlightenment by fortune telling or by holding a seance.

2. After the death of the living Buddha, lamas of the temple would locate the new born that conforms to the conditions laid down in the will. It is likely to locate a number of such boys, but

only one can be chosen. Then all kinds of tests would be conducted, including intelligence, body, appearance and inspiration, to fix the nominees and in the end, one would be chosen by drawing lots.

3. The system of drawing lots from the golden urn has become established for the reincarnation of Dalai and Panchen lamas. In 1793, as part of an effort to turn the tide by overcoming drawbacks characteristic of soul boys nominated from the same tribes, the Qing government promulgated the 29-Article Ordinance for the More Efficient Governing of Tibet. Article one of the Ordinance stipulates: In order to ensure the Yellow Sect continues to flourish, the Grand Emperor bestows it with a golden urn and ivory slips for use in confirming the reincarnated soul boy

◎ After drawing lots from the golden urn, the six-year-old Qoigyijabu in Jiali County, Tibet, was chosen as the reincarnated soul boy of the 10th Panchen Lama to succeed Panchen Erdini to become the 11th Panchen Erdini Qoigyijabu.

of a deceased Living Buddha. Following the lot-drawing ceremony, the High Commissioners and leaders of the soul boy search group are required to report the result to the Central Government. The enthronement ceremony was held following the approval of the Central Government.

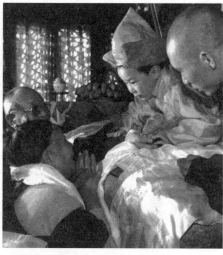

◎ The first Buddhist service of the 11th Panchen Lama in Beijing. On March 9, 1996, the 11th Panchen Erdini Qoigyijabu gave audience to some senior monks, living Buddhas and a host of Buddhism believers at Xihuan Temple in Beijing.

The Qing court commissioned artisans to create two golden urns. One golden urn, used to confirm reincarnations of the Dalai Lama and the Panchen Lama, is currently housed in the Potala Palace in Lhasa. The other, used to confirm the reincarnations of Mongolian and Tibetan Grand Living Buddhas and Hotogtu Living Buddhas, is housed in the Yonghegong Lamasery in Beijing. the names of candidates, as well as their birth years, will be written on the ivory slips in the three languages - Manchu, Han Chinese and Tibetan; the ivory slips will be placed in the golden urn and

◎ On November 22, 1996, Zhao Puchu, Vice-Chairman of the National Committee of CPPCC and President of the Chinese Buddhist Association met the 11th Panchen Erdini Qoigyijabu at Guangji Temple in Beijing.

learned Living Buddhas will pray for seven days before various Hotogtu Living Buddhas and High Commissioners stationed in Tibet by the Central Government officially confirm the reincarnated soul boy by drawing a lot from the golden urn in front of the statue of Sakyamuni in the Jokhang Monastery.

The practice of drawing lots from a golden urn started from the years of Emperor Qian Long of the Qing Dynasty and it later became established. During the period of the nationalist government (1912-1949), the reincarnation of living Buddha had to get the approval from the central government. The reincarnated living Buddhas approved during the Qing dynasty were Grand Living Buddhas of the Monglian and Tibetan systems registered with the Minority Affairs Department, such as Zangjia Hutuketu, Zhebu Zundanpa, Dalai and Panchen.

Living Buddha in Tibetan Buddhism enjoys a high position. He used to be the top leader in the past when the government and religion were unified. He was also the spiritual leader of Buddhism believers. The most influential Living Buddhas in Tibetan Buddhism are Dalai and Panchen.

The 10th Panchen Lama died in Tibet on January 28, 1989. The reincarnated soul boy search group of the Tashilhungbo Monastery spent six years and in the end found three nominees: Gaincain Nobu, Gongsang Wangdui and Arwang Nanzui. The lot drawing ceremony was held in the Jokhang Monastery on November 29, 1995. The State Council sent State Councilor Luo Gan, Jiangcun Luobu, chairman of the Tibet Autonomous Region government and Ye Xiaowen of the State Religious Affairs Bureau to monitor the whole process of drawing lots from the golden urn. Leaders of the Tibetan Party and government organizations, personalities from the Buddhist circles and senior monks of Buddhism from other parts of the country attended the ceremony.

After drawing lots from the golden urn, Qoigyijabu, who was born on Feb. 13, 1990 in Jiali County, Tibet, was chosen as the reincarnated soul boy of the 10th Panchen Lama to succeed Panchen Erdini to become the 11th Panchen Erdini Qoigyijabu.

◎ Golden top Huachang Temple on Mount E'mei.

5. Buddhism education

Since the preaching by five Bhiksus after the death of Sakyamuni, the traditional way of education in Buddhist Temples has lasted for more than 2,000 years. But such a way of education has its limitations for giving a comprehensive training of modern Buddhists.

At the beginning of the 20th century, modern Buddhist education pioneer Master Tai Xu and the noted Buddhism scholar Yang Renshan began to prepare for the founding of a Buddhism university. They paid attention to the training of both monks and know-it-all people. In 1922, Master Tai Xu founded an Institute of Buddhism in Wuchang, Hubei Province and acted as the president, with Liang Qichao serving as the Chairman of the Board of Directors. The Wuchang Institute of Buddhism followed a road that integrated traditional with modern methods of education. It persists in making the law of Buddhism as the fundamental while absorbing the experience of modern Buddhism education at home and abroad. In 1925, the Minnan Institute of

◎ Graduation ceremony of the first study class of the China Buddhism Institute held in September 10, 1959. It is a group photo of the trainees.

Buddhism was founded. Master Tai Xu, who was abbot of Southern Putuo Temple, served as the president.

On August 20, 1932, the Sichuan Institute of Han and Tibetan Buddhism Theories was founded. In 1956, the Buddhist Association of China founded the China Institute of Buddhism in the Fayuan Temple in Beijing. The president of the institute was Shes-rab-rgya-mtsho. This was the first Buddhism institute following the founding of the People's Republic of China and the first regular school of Buddhism before 1980. The institute opened a Han-language class, a specialized class, a regular class

◎ Branch of the Yunnan Provincial Buddhism Institute inside the General Buddhism Temple in Xishuangbanna.

and a postgraduate class.

In September 1961, the institute added a Tibetan-language class. But it did not last long when the Great Cultural Revolution took place in 1966, when all forms of education were paralyzed and the China Institute of Buddhism was also forced to stop. It did not resume class until December 10, 1980. Then it opened a branch school in Lingyan Hill of Suzhou. In December 1984, it added another branch at Qixia Hill. An event of special significance was the opening of a China Tibetan-Language Advanced Buddhism Institute on September 1, 1987. Deng Yingchao (Chairman of the CPPCC National Committee), Xi Zhongxun, Hu Qili and other Party and government leaders attended the inauguration ceremony. The trainees were all living Buddhas and lamas of major temples in areas covered by Tibetan Buddhism. The trainees have a high status in the localities. But as they receive traditional education, they are well versed in Buddhist classics and rituals, but lack the modern general knowledge. Receiving the academic education would help them better cope with all kinds of problems in the modern society. Apart from the Tibetan Advanced Buddhism Institute, another institute devoted to Bali Buddhism was founded in Xishuangbanan of Yunnan province. Up to that time, all the three

◎ Inauguration ceremony of the Quxia Mountain Branch of the China Buddhism Institute.

major lines of Buddhism had their own regular institutes.

The China Institute of Buddhism aims at training senior monks. Under the leadership of the Buddhist Association of China, it has traversed more than 40 years of zigzag road and trained a large number of Buddhists, who have become the backbone forces in China's Buddhism. Over the past 40 years, Shes-rab-rgya-mtshuo, Master Fa Zun, Zhao Puchu and Master Yi Cheng served successively the president of the institute.

The institute has been exploring for and improving teaching and management, resulting in a good style of learning. It requires trainees to develop intelligently and morally and to carry forward and develop the fine tradition of integrating farm work with meditation, carrying out academic studies and international exchanges. The institute has introduced the integration of learning and self-cultivation and encourages bush life of both students and monks, advocates for trisiksa or three studies, namely, the study of commandment, samathi (intent contemplation) and wisdom, in addition to literature, history and philosophy, law and policies toward religion.

The institute has become a window for friendly exchanges with Buddhists in other countries. Over the past half century, visiting the institute were Buddhists from India, Cambodia, Sri

◎ A group photo of the second group of Buddhistsof Southern Fujian Institute of Buddhism accompanying the relics of the Buddha for exhibition in Taiwan.

Lanka, Thailand, Viet Nam, Laos, Nepal, Myanmar, the United States, Japan, Singapore, the Republic of Korea and the Democratic People's Republic of Korea. The institute has also tightened its ties with Buddhist disciples in Hong Kong, Macau and Taiwan.

The China Advanced Tibetan-Language Buddhism Institute was founded in Xihuang Lamasery on September 1, 1987 under the sponsorship of the Tenth Panchen Lama and China's Buddhist Association president Zhao Puchu.

Xihuang Lamasery is a well-known temple of Tibetan Buddhism, enjoying a high prestige in history. It is equivalent to the official residence of Dalai and Panchen lamas. The lamasery was built in 1652, when the 5th Dalai Lama led more than 3,000 monks on a 9-month journey from Tibet to Xihuang in Beijing. Since then, when Dalai and Panchen lamas came to Beijing, they would stay there.

There is a Panchen stupa in the Xihuang Lamasery, where the clothes and hat of the 6th Panchen Lama are kept. The stone stupa was built by Emperor Qian Long of the Qing Dynasty in memory of the 6th Panchen Lama. The body of the stupa is made of marble, carved with such exquisite patterns of Buddhist images, images of Bodhisattva, figurines, flowers and animals

◎ Tranquil Pagoda at Xihuang Temple in Beijing.

symbolizing luck. Featuring the blend of Indian and Tibetan architectural styles, the Xihuang Lamasery is held up as the cream of Tibetan Buddhist architectural arts and sculptural arts.

The institute is a comprehensive institute of higher learning specializing in Buddhism, supplemented by other disciplines. The students are reincarnations of living Buddhas and young monks from Tibet, Qinghai, Sichuan, Gansu, Yunnan, Inner Mongolia and Xinjiang.

6. Buddhist culture

Buddhism is an alien religion and it has brought in alien culture. In the long history of its spread in China, the alien Buddhist culture and China's local culture got infused to become part of the traditional Chinese culture. In recent 20-30 years, Buddhists, scientists and even political figures have all become aware of the special features of Buddhist culture and the conceptual differences between the religion of Buddhism and Buddhist culture. This has stimulated the inheritance and development of Buddhist culture and injected renewed life into it.

BUDDHIST SCRIPTURE PRINTING

The printing of Buddhist scriptures is both an undertaking for spreading Buddhism and Buddhist culture. The ancient printing technique is of special significance in carrying over traditional culture. At present, such techniques are still adopted in the printing of the original versions of scriptures at Jinling Scripture Engraving Service, the rubbing print of the Buddhist stone inscriptions at Yunju Monastery in Fangshan and the wood-block printing of Tibetan Buddhist scriptures at Dege Buddhist Press.

(1). JINLING BUDDHIST PRESS

Situated in Nanjing City, Jiangsu Province, the Jinling Buddhist Press is an ancient site for printing Buddhist scriptures manually by using engraved blocks. It is also an institution for studying Buddhism. The press was started by Upsaka Yang Renshan in the mid-19th century. Yang Renshan made his own residence as a Buddhist press, working there for more than 40

◎ Scripture print blocks kept by the Jinling Buddhist Press.

years. He engraved more than 47,000 blocks, forming a treasure-house of wooden-block scripture versions. It is also a place for Buddhist education and Buddhism studies for more than 100 years. The scriptures printed were all proof-read by Yang Renshan and other noted Buddhism scholars at the time.

During the Great Cultural Revolution (1966-1976), the Jinling Buddhist Press was destroyed and the more than 100,000 printing blocks were stamped to pieces. The printing press did not resume until 1981. Over the past 20 years, the printing press has restored more than 120,000 printing blocks. The classic thread-bound books printed by the press have become very popular among Buddhist disciples at home and abroad and among cultural circles. The 90-year-old Tiantai Sect Patriarch in Japan visited the press, saying that "this is your national treasure and also national treasure of ours".

(2). STONE BUDDHIST SCRIPTURES AT YUNJU MONASTERY IN FANGSHAN

Amidst high mountains 75 kilometers southwest of Beijing, there is a Yunju Temple. To the southwest of the temple, there is a pagoda where relics of Sakyamuni are kept. In a cave under the pagoda are kept 10082 stone blocks on which are carved scriptures. Nine other stone caves in the surrounding all have stone scriptures, totaling 4978 blocks. It is said that the scriptures were carved by senior monk Jing Wan of the Sui Dynasty. He carved Buddhist scriptures on stone blocks in order to prevent the repetition of destruction of Buddhism in history. In the past, Buddhist scriptures were mostly printed on paper, very easy to be destroyed. Senior Monk Jing Wan carved the Buddhist scriptures on stone and hid them in mountain caves so that they would be passed on. Starting from the Sui Dynasty, people continued carving the scriptures for more than 1000 years through the Tang, Song, Liao, Jin, Yuan, Ming and Qing dynasties. This

◎ Text of stone Buddhist scripture at Yunju Monastery in Fangshan, Beijing.

◎ Fangshan Buddhist Scripture Hill.

is a miracle in the history of human civilization and an event that merits singing in the history of Chinese culture.

In 1956, the China Buddhist Association started to sort out and make rubbing copies of the stone scriptures hidden in mountain caves. More than 30,000 rubbings were made and numbered. The China Buddhism Books and Historical Relics Library under the China Buddhist Association has made unremitting efforts to study and sort out the scriptures and published 34 titles of photo-print hard copies, which are held up

◎ The stone scriptures put back to the stone cave again in order to protect them from being eroded. The photo shows a Buddhist service for returning the scriptures to the stone cave held at Yunju Temple on September 9, 1999.

as the treasure of Chinese culture.

In 1999, the Yunju Temple put the more than 10,000 stone blocks of Buddhist scriptures back to the caves with a grand religious service.

(3). DEGE BUDDHIST PRESS

Dege Buddhist Press is one of the largest Buddhist scripture printing centers in China. Situated inside the Gengqing Monastery in Dege County, Sichuan Province, the printing press was built in 1729 by Tusi of Dege. It occupies a floor space of more than

1,600 square meters, with a dozen Tibetan style rooms. In history, it was a Buddhist press parallel with those in the Potala Palace and Xigaze, known as three Tibetan Buddhist presses. It is the only such press survived. It now has a collection of more than 217,000 blocks for class books on Buddhism in the Tibetan language and a few blocks for picture books. The press has printed 586 copies in 82 volumes of translated books on biography, history, literature, arts, medicine, astrology and calendar. The most famous among them are "Bak-gyur", "Bstanggyur", "Sakya Encyclopedia", "Four Classics of Medicine", "Collection of

◎ Print block ware house of Dege Buddhist press.

Medical Works", "Royal Chronicle of Tibet", "Collection of Zongkapa"(Asuns-hbum) and "Origin of Tibetan Buddhism". The classic works have been distributed not only in Tibet, Sichuan, Yunnan and Gansu but also in India, Japan, Nepal, Southeast Asia and Western Europe.

7. Buddhist Caves

Buddhist caves were introduced into China's central area following the spread of Buddhism. The statues and murals in the caves represent the most important treasure house of Buddhist arts. They are not only the cultural legacy of China but also an important part of the world cultural legacy. The most representative are the Dunhuang Grottoes, Yungang Grottoes, Longmen Grottoes and Maijishan Grottoes.

DUNHUANG GROTTOES

Dunhuan Grottoes are the Mogao Caves inside Dunhuan County, Gansu Province. It is also known as One Thousand Buddha Caves, carved out of the rocks along the eastern side of the Mingsha Hill, 25 km southeast of Dunhuang. Work started in 366 and continued through the Northern Wei, Western Wei, Northern Zhou, Sui, Tang, Five Dynasties, Song, Western Xia and Yuan. Despite erosion and destruction, 492 caves have been well preserved, with frescoes covering an area of 45,000 square

◎ Outer view of Dunhuang Grottoes.

meters, more than 2,000 colored sculptured figures.

Dunhuang is situated in the westernmost end of the Gansu Corridor. It used to be an important town on the ancient Silk Road, an inevitable road for economic and cultural exchanges between the west and the east. Some of the caves are the central pillar caves influenced by Caitya cave of India and some are Chinese style caves. The caves are not used for meditation but for enshrining the Buddha and Bodhisattvas. The shape of the cave appeared toward the end of the Northern Wei Dynasty and continued into the Yuan, with only slight changes in the shapes and positions of niches. As the areas are sandy, carving was difficult. So sculptures and murals are quite developed. Most of the sculptures are colorful. There are more than 1,400 sculptured statues well preserved in Mogao Grottoes. There are also more than 70 incomplete ones and 720 were repaired ones. The biggest stands 15 meters and the smallest stands some 20 centimeters. Although made for more than 1,000 years, the sculptures are still as hard as rock and fresh in color. The earliest sculptures were made in the Northern Wei Dynasty, which are similar to Indian in style, with high and straight noses, clear demarcation of brows and eyes and spiraling hair knots, looking very solemn. Colors include white, brown and green. The sculptures are leaning

◎ Sculpture of Dunhuang Grottoes.

against cave walls, giving an impression of relief carving. Up to the Sui Dynasty, the slim figures became fatter, with flabby faces and big ears. The color painting became more exquisite and the wears also looked more colorful, with the folds and veins of clothes soft and clear. The images of Bodhisattva with bare bust and arms are mostly females, looking tranquil, beautiful, symbolizing charm and wisdom. Although the exposed parts are small, they look refined and smooth. Masculine men show strong muscles, showing great strength. The clothes and decorations are natural and silky to touch.

Many of the murals were destroyed due to sandstorms and

◎ Dazu stone sculpptures.

scorching sun as well as by natural disasters and wars. Some caves have disappeared altogether. There are only 492 caves and 450,000 square meters of murals well preserved. The murals, if spread out, may extend to as long as 30 kilometers. They present different styles during different historical periods. The mural paintings in existence today can be divided into seven categories, including the jataka stories depicting beneficence of Sakyamuni in his previous incarnations, sutra stories depicting suffering and transmigration, and traditional Chinese mythology.

Images of Buddhist scriptures are the main body of mural designs. There are now more than 120 murals on the pure land in the west. But there were not many in the early period. During the Northern Wei Dynasty, there were only jataka stories, devil conquering stories and nirvana, mostly simple stories. Up to the Sui dynasty, subjects of images of Buddhist scriptures began to increase. Up to the Tang Dynasty (618-907), the scripture stories assumed a joyful and enthusiastic style. But such images began to be formalized during the Song Dynasty (960-1279), marking the end of the hey-days.

Jataka stories mainly depict benevolence of Sakyamuni in his previous incarnations.

Respected images. They include the Buddha, bodhisattvas, arhats, lesser thousand Buddhas and preaching images. The most attractive is the "flying angels" that flies with two floating ribbons.

Patron images: They refer to images of those who spent the money building the caves. They include both nobles and the mean.

The caves carved on the cliff walls provide voluminous research material for the study of all aspects of Chinese medieval society, in areas such as religion, art, politics, economics, military affairs, culture, literature, language, music, dance, architecture and medical science. In 1900, the 26th year of the reign of Emperor Guang Xu, a Buddhist scripture cave was discovered and more than 40,000 Buddhist scriptures, books and other relics were kept. The major discovery has given birth to a new field of study, "Dunhuangology" in the world.

YUNGANG GROTTOES

Located at the southern foot of Wuzhou Mountain some 16 km west of Datung City, Shanxi Province, Yungang Grottoes is built against the mountain, extending about 1 km (0.62 miles) from east to west. The construction of the caves started under the auspices of the noted monk Tan Yao in 453 and took 50 years to complete. Some 40,000 people, including Buddhists from what is present Sri Lanka, contributed to the huge project.

The 53 caves in Yungang Grottoes include some 1,000 niches with about 51,000 statues - a treasure-trove of cave art that combines traditional Chinese art forms with foreign influence, particularly Greek and Indian. Sculptures here are noted for their vigorous features and rich variety that range from the smallest, only 2 centimeters high, to the tallest - a Buddha 17-meters high. The tallest Buddha is surrounded by many small Buddhas in Cave No. 5, also called the Big Buddha Cave.

The Yungang Grottoes are divided into three zones: east, west and central, numbered from east to west. Caves No.1 and No. 2 are located in the east zone. Statues and sculptures inside

◎   Outer view of Yungang Grottoes.

these caves have been severely damaged by exposure to the elements, but still preserved in the east zone are relief sculptures of Buddhist stories on the lower part of the eastern wall of Cave No. 1. Inside the entrance of the Yungang Temple is an impressive four-storeyed wooden facade with glazed top outside Caves No. 3, 4 and 5.

Most of the caves are in the western zone, and each has its own character. Cave No. 20 - one of the five earliest caves of monk Tan Yao - houses the sitting statue of Sakyamuni, 13.7 meters high, with a full and round face wearing a majestic smile, slim lips and a high nose, ears that extend almost to the shoulders, radiant eyes and broad shoulders. Sakyamuni statue is representative of Buddha sculptures in Yungang Grottoes.

LONGMEN GROTTOES

The Longmen Grottoes, located 13km from Luoyang, Henan Province, are a treasure house of ancient Buddhist cave art. The grottoes were hewed and carved during the Northern Wei Dynasty (386-534), when the rulers relocated their capital at Luoyang near the end of the 5th century. The construction of the Longmen Grottoes began in 493 during the reign of Emperor Xiao Wen and continued through the successive six dynasties, including

Northern Wei, Western Wei, Northern Qi, Sui, Tang and Northern Song, lasting for more than 500 years. One third of the caves were dug during the Northern Wei Dynasty and two-thirds were

◎ Buddhist image at Fengguang Temple at Longmen.

carved during the Tang Dynasty. Altogether there are more than 2,100 niches, more than 100,000 statues of the Buddha, Bodhisattvas, and Arhats, and 3,600 inscribed stone tablets along the 1-km-long cliff of Mt. Longmen on the west and Mt.

Xiangshan on the east of the Yihe River.

MAIJISHAN GROTTOES

This mountain in modern Gansu province was first used as a Buddhist refuge at the end of 4th century. Although Maijishan is not as famous as the above three grottoes, the grottoes in this curious mountain contain more than 7,000 Buddha and Bodhisattva steles.

The Maijishan Mountain is named after its shape like a haystack. The grottoes of this mountain contain very beautiful

© Distant view of Maijishan Grottoes.

◎ Manjusri (Western Wei Period) in a niche on the right of No. 123 cave at Maijishan Grottoes.

statues of Bodhisattvas like the left Pusa whose face lineaments are very soft, almost like that of a girl.

The Maijishan Grottoes are the best preserved, as the caves were dug from the precipices of rock mountain and the wooden path leading to the caves was destroyed.

In 2003, the China Buddhist Culture Institute and the Maijishan Arts Institute jointly published a picture book "Maijishan, Kingdom of Buddhism" to recapture the history, current conditions and sculptural arts of the Maijishan Grottoes.

Besides, the Dazu (big foot) Grottoes in Sichuan Province and Jianchuan Grottoes all have their unique artistic styles.

8. Buddhist Architecture

The earliest Buddhist structure that spread into China from India was called "Buddhist Cave Temple" or "meditation caves". When Indian monks Kasyapamatanga and Dharmaranya came to Luoyang to spread Buddhism, they did not have time to study how to build Buddhist temples in China and they used official offices as service sites. All these official offices were named as so-and-so temples, such as Honglu Temple, Taichang Temple.

◎ Buddhist cave

Temple thus became Buddhist service sites.

Chinese have a strong sense of city walls and moats. The imperial palace was walled in and even official residences were surrounded by high walls. Temples, too, have high walls, just like official residences. All the structures are arranged along a central axis, with subsidiary halls flanking the central axis. Later on, in order to keep away from secular life, temples were built in scenic spots in mountain forests. Temples planted lotus flowers and built pools for monks to release captive animals and living things, such as shrimps and turtles to exhibit their kind-hearted spirit. The temples also planted Bodhi tree or other trees of religious significance. By and

© Buddhist Temple in Suzhou Garden.

by, temples became scenic spots for tourists. There is a Chinese saying: "Most of the beautiful mountains are occupied by monks." Wherever there are beautiful landscapes there are Buddhist temples. Nowadays, a temple serves as a Buddhist service site, a park and a tourist spot.

In recent years, many new temples have been built. A new temple, called Nanshan Temple was built at the southernmost end of the Hainan Island, serving as a park, a Buddhist service site and a natural landscape of the sea. The Xiangfu Temple and Open-air Buddha built in Wuxi also serve as temples and gardens. It is true with the Yufo Temple in Anshan of Liaoning Province, Northeast China.

9. Buddhist Music

Buddhist music appeared in the times of the Buddha. At that time, Buddhist disciples often used music and dances or the so-called "Sanskrit Music", originally as a form of Buddhist chant accompanied by simple ceremonial instruments to glorify and eulogize the Buddha and bodhisattvas. When it was brought into China, there were some problems of disharmony between the language and rhythm and it was not completely accepted in China. But after being adopted by the Chinese Buddhists, it embodied the features of Chinese traditional music, thus causing the Sanskrit music developed in China to have a greater variation in style and contents. The music itself is of utmost tranquility which uplifts the mind and spirit to transcendence. Most of the tunes were transplanted from operas and music numbers, folk music and chamber music. Only the words were created. In the 1930s, noted senior monk Master Taixu created the "Song of Triratna" and it was at that time that Buddhist musical creation began.

In the 1950s, a number of noted national musicians turned

© Monks at Zhihua Temple performing Buddhist musical pieces.

their eyes to Buddhist music and collected, sorted out, studied and preserved Buddhist music. A typical example is the study of the music of the Zhihua Temple in Beijing, which has a history of more than 500 years. Zhihua Temple was built in the Ming Dynasty. It used to be a family temple of Wang Zhen, a favorite eunuch of the emperor. It was said that the temple introduced the secular music from the imperial palace to be played by the monks. For more than 500 years, the ancient music numbers have been passed on for 26-27 generations. The Zhihua Temple has preserved a large number of materials on ancient music and objects.

In 1980 when the music in the temple was on the verge of extinction, the Beijing Buddhist Association began to launch a fresh round of rescuing operation. It called back artistic monks scattered in all parts of the country and recalled the musical numbers and had them recorded in tapes. In 1984, the temple gave its first concert. In 1986, the Beijing Buddhist Music Troupe was founded. Not long ago, the music troupe went on a seven-city tour of Germany, France and Switzerland. Then, the music troupe went on to tour Singapore, Belgium, Taiwan and Hong Kong. Following its suit, many temples founded their own Buddhist music troupes. Noted among them are Wutai Mountain Buddhist Music Troupe, the Labrang Monastery Music Troupe and Qianshan Buddhist Music Troupe. In November 2003, a number of Buddhist music troupes and a Buddhist Sanskrit Music Troupe held large scaled concerts in Shanghai and Beijing.

In recent years, all kinds of Buddhist music CDs and tapes have appeared on the market. The creation of Buddhist music is in for a flourishing period.

10. Buddhist publications

The first Buddhist magazine "Modern Buddhism" appeared in China in 1950. It became the journal of the China Buddhist Association in 1954. It was suspended in the Great Cultural Revolution period of 1966-1976. In 1981, the China Buddhist Association began to publish a new journal "The Sound of the Law". Now it is distributed nationwide and to a dozen other countries and regions. After 1987, the magazine "Buddhist Culture" launched by the China Buddhist Cultural Institute came into being. The journal stresses the spread of Buddhist culture and arts. In the 1990s, all places began to launch some new journals on Buddhism. The most influential among them are

◎ Buddhist publications.

◎ Picture books and memorial books compiled and published by China Buddhist Association and China Buddhist Cultural Institute.

"Shanghai Buddhism", "Guangdong Buddhism", "Tibetan Buddhism", "Luoyang Buddhism", "Human World" and "Meditation". Some institutes of Buddhism also have their own gazettes, such as "Sources of the Law" by the China Institute of Buddhism, the "Gazette of Southern Fujian Buddhism Institute", "Sweet Dew" by the Jiuhuashan Buddhism Institute, and "Gazette of Shanghai Institute of Buddhism". All publishing houses have also published books on Buddhism.

The Chinese Buddhist Association and the China Buddhism Culture Institute often hold exhibitions on Buddhist culture to make public such historical materials on Buddhist activities in ancient times. They also held exhibitions in Australia and Singapore.

11. Buddhist Dances

Buddhist dance, just like Buddhist music, is a means of spreading the doctrines of Buddhism and an offering to the Buddha. The subjects of dances are very popular. In Tibetan Buddhism, there is a dance called "the Dance of Law". It is a masked dance. When the body of a dancer shakes, it is called "Qian mu" and when only the arms of the dancer wave, it is called "Tar". It was recorded

◎ Tibetan Buddhist Dance.

that the dance came from the Vajira section of Yoga. The purpose of organizing Icham service is to drive away ghosts, make contributions to the god and celebrate Buddhist image eye opening. Sometimes, when the translation of Buddhist scriptures was finished, monks also performed masked dances.

◎ Icham or driving away devils dance of Tibetan Buddhism.

In Labrang Monastery of Gansu Province, the Dance of Law is usually performed on the 14th day of the first month in the lunar calendar, at the beginning of March and on the 15th day of the third month and the 29th day of the ninth month. At the Yonghegong Lamasery in Beijing, there is a dance called Icham. All the dances mentioned above belong to what is called "Qiangmu" of the Tibetan Buddhism. Lamas at Yonghegong Lamasery perform the dance for three days starting from the 29th day of the first month of the lunar calendar.

The so-called Icham or driving away devils is to drive away

◎ Han-language Buddhist dance.

all temptations and obstacles to cultivation. The masks the dancers wear including lion, tiger, elephant, leopard, cow, dog and dear. There are also human shaped masks. Only monks are allowed to perform such a dance and the dance is not allowed to be performed on non-religious occasions. But, to a certain extent, the performance of Icham has also become part of the life of common people. Whenever it is performed, it attracts a large crowd.

The dances of Southern Buddhism are mainly dances of the Dai people. Dai people are good at singing and dancing. When Southern Buddhism was introduced into Dai nationality, dances with Buddhism subjects began to flourish. As all Dai people believe in Buddhism, all their activities have the influence of Buddhism. Dances of Southern Buddhism are quite different from Tibetan Buddhism. Tibetan Buddhism dances are performed by monks but Southern Buddhism does not allow monks to sing and dance. Tibetan Buddhism dances are part of religious rites while Southern Buddhism dances reflect more of secular life and can be performed on any occasion. Subjects of Buddhism dances include life story of Sakyamuni.

The "Peacock Dance" was originated in "Jataka (stories of Buddha's previous incarnation). Now the religious colors of the dance have been weakened. It has become a representative dance

◎ Southern Buddhist dance.

of the Dai people. On September 23, 2003, the Yunnan Miaoyin Song and Dance Ensemble performed "Presenting Heart Lamp to the Buddha" during the celebrations of the 50th Anniversary of the founding of the Chinese Buddhist Association. Holding lotus shaped candles and wearing long nails, the dancers danced to the company of drums and musical instruments, exhibiting the artistic fascination of Buddhist arts.

12. Buddhist Paintings

Chinese Buddhist paintings are originated in India. At the beginning, they were painted on walls of stone caves, which were introduced to China's inland. At the beginning, Chinese knew little about the alien religion. Buddhist murals helped people understand more about Buddhism. The murals of Kezer cave, Dunhuang Cave, Guizi cave and Bingling Temple caves and Maijishan caves all come from Buddhist scriptures. But later on, Buddhist paintings were not confined to

◎ Mural of Han-language Buddhism.

◎ Murual of Tibetan Buddhism.

murals, but the subjects remained. When the Chan Sect culture rose, meditation paintings came into being. There were a number of meditation painters.

Toward the end of the 20th century, there was a famous painter named Huichan Master (Xu Guoliang in secular name). He painted many traditional Chinese paintings with Buddhist doctrines as the subject matter. His attempt was of special significance. Buddhism covers two aspects. One is believers and the other is subject of belief. Believers are Buddhist disciples while the subjects of belief are the Buddha and bodhisattvas. In the long history, believers used all kinds of art forms to portray subjects of belief. As most of the images of the Buddha and bodhisattvas were standardized by authoritative Buddhist scriptures, the established images took a big part of the paintings. Believer

◎ Partial view of the painting "Mother" created by Master Huichan.

seldom had works to portray them.

Huichan Master of Law zeroed in on the pious Buddhist believers at the very beginning. In order to portray believers immersed in the religious world, heart and soul, Huichan Master also poured his pure feeling into portraying them. He viewed his works with an eye of a Buddhist instead of an ordinary painter. One of his works before he became a monk, "Scripture Engravers", won a grand prize at the 23rd Monte Carlo International modern arts fair.

13. Charity

Taking pleasure in doing good and giving in charity is a tradition of Chinese Buddhists. Such virtue is the "fine tradition of Buddhism". In 1952, Chairman Mao Zedong raised the slogan of "carrying forward the fine tradition of Buddhism". Chinese Buddhist circles have been active in giving in charity and undertaking public welfare, disaster and poverty relief, giving out medicine and treating patients, constructing roads and bridges, planting trees, aiding drop-out students, running homes for the aged, helping the handicapped and rescuing wild animals. The noted Buddhist charity organization is the Nanputuo Charity Fund. The organization was founded according to the will of Master Miao Zhen before his death: "Don't forget that there are still many people suffering in the world". The fund has developed in strength in recent years under the leadership of Master Sheng Hui, President of the Chinese Buddhist Association. The targets of relief are scattered in all parts of the country. It has also helped local Buddhist associations establish dozens of charity

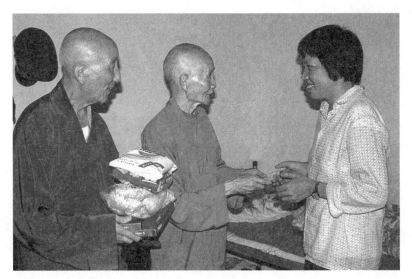

◎ Master Weixian and Master Xinyue of the Charity Society donating food to people in difficulty.

organizations. Over the past eight years, the Nanputuo Charity Fund donated more than 17 million yuan to help build 19 "Hope Schools" and undertakings in addition to poverty and disaster victim relief.

The Chongqing Municipal Buddhist Association set up a Hope School Committee and then a special Charity Society. Over the past 10 years, the committee aided more than 24,000 dropouts. In 1998, it carried out activities to aid poor mothers and their children. The Guangdong Buddhist Association has over the past ten years devoted more than 100 million yuan to charity. Now there are six charity funds, one home for the aged and one home for abandoned babies. The Shanghai Buddhist Association has two special funds, which have over the past 20 years donated more than 16 million yuan. Hunan is a province where charity undertakings are the best run.

14. Friendship ties with Hong Kong, Macao and Taiwan Buddhist Circles

The Buddhist circles on the Chinese mainland have always kept close ties with Buddhist organizations in Hong Kong, Macao and Taiwan, especially after China carried out reform and opening-up policies. Of the most prominent of all exchanges, two major events are extraordinary. One is the building of the Tiantan Buddha and the other is the movement of the relics of Sakyamuni from the Famen Temple in Shaanxi to Taiwan.

When hearing that Hong Kong was to build a giant bronze Buddhist statue by the Baolian Temple on the Lantau Island in Hong Kong, Zhao Puchu, President of the Chinese Buddhist Association jumped upon the idea and organized a special committee to raise 5 million yuan as contributions to the building of the statue.

On February 23, 2002, part of the relics of Sakyamuni at Famen Temple of Fufeng County, Shaanxi Province, was sent to Taiwan via Hong Kong in the company of 400 Buddhists. The

◎ Eye-opening ceremony of the completion of the Tiantan Buddhist Image on December 29, 1993.

◎ Grand service, welcoming the figure bone relic in Kaohsiung, Taiwan on the afternoon of March 30, 2002.

relic of Sakyamuni is a section of a finger bone kept at Famen Temple. It is a valuable national treasure. It has been kept there for more than 1000 years. During the Tang dynasty, the relic was taken to the imperial court on six occasions for worshiping. Now, more than 1000 years later, the Buddha relic was sent to Taiwan with a ceremony never witnessed before. It was worshiped for 37 days in Taiwan and millions of people paid homage to it. The event was held up as a harbinger of the heydays of the Chinese nation as in the Tang period.

15. Foreign Exchanges

Chinese Buddhist circles have close relations with those of Japan and the Republic of Korea.

The Han-language Buddhism was spread to the Korea Peninsula toward the end of the 3rd century, when there were three kingdoms there: Paekche, Koguryo and Silla.

At about 6th century, Chinese Buddhism found its way to Japan. But now many scholars deemed the date much earlier. But the commonly recognized time is 538, when a king of the state of Baiji presented to the Japanese emperor with a golden statue of Sakyamuni and some scriptures. Linked by Buddhism, China, Korea Peninsula and Japanese Islands enjoy special relationship. For more than 1000 years, there have been frequent exchanges by Buddhists among them. Zhao Puchu called it a "golden bond".

The Republic of Korea (ROK) was late in establishing diplomatic ties with China and so the restoration of the exchanges between Buddhists was delayed. In August 1990, the Chinese

◎ First Conference on friendly exchanges among China, the Republic of Korea and Japan held at the Beijing International Conference Center in Beijing on May 22, 1995.

Buddhist Association extended an official invitation to the ROK Buddhist organization. In October 1990, a Chinese Buddhist delegation visited Seoul and attended the 17th World Buddhist Friendship Conference. After the establishment of diplomatic relations in 1992, the exchanges between Buddhist circles of the two countries have been frequent, several times a year.

The relations between Buddhist circles of China and Japan were hurt during the Second World War. In 1952, when the Asian and Pacific Peace Conference was held in China, the Chinese delegation presented a Buddha image to the Japanese delegation.

◎ Second conference of friendly exchanges among China, the Republic of Korea and Japan held in Seoul in September 1996.

After receiving the Buddha image, the Japanese Buddhists sent a message to the preparatory committee for the establishment of the Chinese Buddhist Association, expressing regret for failing to stop Japanese militarists from invading China, thus bringing untold sufferings to the Chinese people. One of the concrete actions of Japanese Buddhists for restoring the traditional friendship was the event of sending back the remains of Chinese armymen captured by Japan. From 1955, many friendship organizations were set up in Japan. In April, 1980, the statue of Chinese senior monk Jian Zhen, which had been enshrined in a

Japanese temple, was sent to China for exhibition. This non-governmental activity was of great significance, which went far beyond religious activities. It, in fact, became a positive factor for the normalization of diplomatic relations between the two countries. The ancestral homes of all sects of Buddhism are in China. The Chinese Buddhist Association has invested a lot of money in having these temples repaired and rebuilt. The temples where Japanese monks preached have also been well protected. Some temples have set up memorial halls for Japanese monks, such as in Ningbo, Zhaoqing of Guangdong, Xi'an and Shanxi.

◎ Third conference of friendly exchanges among China, the Republic of Korea and Japan held in Kyodo, Japan, in October 1997.

Buddhism has, in fact, become a "golden bridge" for the friendly exchanges among China, Japan and the Republic of Korea, just as President Zhao Puchu said during his visit to Japan in 1993. President Zhao expressed the hope that Buddhists of the three countries would carry forward the tradition of friendship and cooperation established from ancient times and let this "golden bridge" link more countries and nations and contribute to the prosperity and stability of Asia and to world peace and happiness.

On May 22, 1995, the first meeting of Buddhists of China, Japan and the Republic of Korea was held in Beijing. The meeting adopted a "Beijing Declaration", calling for highest alert against the repetition of historical tragedy, which referred to Japanese invasion of the Republic of Korea and China. The meeting decided to hold such exchange alternatively in China, Japan and the Republic of Korea. The second such exchange was held in Seoul in 1996 and the third was held in Kyodo, Japan. Every exchange had the participation of nearly one thousand people.

In 2001, the three-party conference was held in Beijing and held a photo exhibition on environmental protection in the eyes of Buddhists.

Chinese Buddhist Association has also developed good

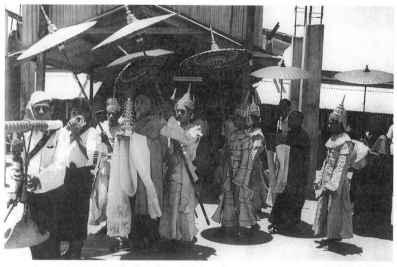

© Myanmar Buddhists holding grand ceremony to welcome Chinese Buddhist delegation to the conference hall. Chinese delegation leader Sherab Gyamtso presented Buddhist relics, Buddhist scriptures and mantle and alms bowl to the Buddhist circle of Myanmar.

relations with Buddhists in other Asian countries.

On November 24, 1956, a grand ceremony was held in New Delhi, India, on the occasion of the 2500th anniversary of the death of the Buddha. The Chinese Buddhist Association participated in the preparations for the ceremony.

In his greetings to the Chinese Buddhists over the national radio, Zhao Puchu reminded the Chinese Buddhists of never forgetting the exchanges with Buddhists of Korea, Japan, Vietnam, Nepal and Laos. He called on Chinese Buddhists to model on the great Buddha and devote their efforts to eliminating wars and contribute to friendship and peace in the world.

Chinese Buddhists have had several major exchanges with their fellow Buddhists of Myanmar since the founding of New China. The first was the exhibition of the teeth of the Buddha in the capital of Myanmar in 1955. Grand ceremonies were held when the Buddha's relic was taken to Myanmar and when it was taken back. The second exhibition was held in 1994. From 1996 to 1997, the Buddha relic was exhibited in Myanmar on three occasions. The exhibition was held in eight provinces, 9 cities

◎ Master Dabei, permanent council member of the Chinese Buddhist Association and Abbot of Guangji Temple, accepting the precious gifts from Ceylon Buddhist circles on July 28, 1957.

◎ Living Buddha of the China Senior Buddhism Institute visiting the Ulan-Ude Kampo Monastery of the Buryat Republic of Russia.

and 15 administrative areas in Myanmar, receiving more than three million visitors. For scores of years, the Buddha's relic has become a bridge of friendship between China and Myanmar.

In 1956, a 15-member Chinese Buddhist delegation headed by Sherab Gyamtso participated in the Fourth World Buddhist Conference in Nepal. During the visit, the Chinese delegation donated 10,000 lubi for restoring Lumbini. In 1986, Zhao Puchu and Master Panchen participated in the 15th World Buddhist Friendship Conference. At the meeting, Master Panchen announced that China would build a Buddhist temple in Lumbini as part of the Lumbini development program. Not long after, the work on the temple, named "All-China Temple" started. It was completed in 1999. The monumental work has become another historical witness to the friendly exchanges between Chinese Buddhists and Buddhists of South Asia.

图书在版编目（CIP）数据

中国佛教／凌海成著．—北京：五洲传播出版社，2004.6

（中国宗教基本情况丛书）

ISBN 7-5085-0535-2

Ⅰ.中… Ⅱ.凌… Ⅲ.佛教史－中国－英文 Ⅳ.B949.2

中国版本图书馆 CIP 数据核字（2004）第 050777 号

《中国佛教》

责任编辑：荆孝敏

编辑助理：蔡　程

图片提供：凌海成　桑　吉等

设计承制：北京紫航文化艺术有限公司

翻译：金绍卿

《中国佛教》

五洲传播出版社

地址：中国北京北三环中路 31 号　邮编：100088

电话：82008174 网址：www.cicc.org.cn

开本：140×210　1/32　印张：9

2004 年 6 月第一版　印数 1-7000

ISBN 7-5085-0535-2／B·42

定价：48.00 元